Anna Mancini

The Meaning

Of

Dreams

Buenos Books AMERICA

© 2007 by Anna Mancini.
All rights reserved.

No part of this book may be reproduced, stored in a retrieval system, or transmitted by any means, electronic, mechanical, photocopying, recording, or otherwise, without written permission from the author.

PAPERBACK: ISBN : 978-1-932848-43-4

2d edition revised of the Intelligence of dreams

www.buenosbooks.us

info@buenosbooks.us

CONTENTS

INTRODUCTION 5
Chapter 1: The body at the meeting-point between dreams and reality 9
   1. A body of unexplored ancient knowledge about Man 9
   2. The body as a bridge between the tangible and the intangible 10
   3. The body as a transmitter and receiver of information 11
Chapter 2: How to observe the connections between your dreams and your reality 21
   1. How to observe your dreaming process 21
   2. How to record your dreams 23
   3. How to take notes about your waking life 32
Chapter 3: Some of the results achieved thanks to this method of observation 35
   1. Understanding energy exchanges between people and with the environment 35
   2. A different approach to space-time 41
   3. A different approach to medicine 48
Chapter 4: How you can use the dream-reality connections 57
   1. A powerful tool for accessing information 57
   2. Using the dream-reality connection to improve your life 58
   3. Accelerating the path of scientific innovation 59
   4. Avoiding obstructions to the good functioning of your dream process 61
Chapter 5: A new philosophy of mind 63
   1. What makes our brain work? 63

2. Which capacities of the conscious mind energize us the most?.. 64
3. The collective awakening of a different kind of intelligence 67
Conclusion.. 71
Frequently asked questions 75
BIBLIOGRAPHY 89
NOTES 93

INTRODUCTION

Life on earth is impossible without a mix of matter and energy, without a body and its intangible life force. Despite the necessity of both the tangible and the intangible, humanity has always focused only on one aspect of life to the detriment of the other. History shows that human societies have always made a selection: they have applied their attention either to the material or to the immaterial side of life, and excluded the other dimension. This is why today we still find so-called "primitive" societies coexisting with so-called "civilized" ones. The first have focused their attention on the intangible, and have developed the corresponding brain capacities. The second have focused their attention on the tangible world, and have developed a different set of brain capacities needed for that purpose. The study of the dream process, a universal phenomenon, did not escape this divide. And this is why we have not yet come to understand what dreams are, their utility and how much they can help us improve our waking life. Dreams are at the heart of a process where tangible and intangible worlds are intimately intermingled. Indeed, a dream is an intangible phenomenon occurring in a physical body that stands in an environment both material and informational (intangible). A systematic investigation of the connections between dreams and reality sheds new light on the dream process and on the functioning of the mind. This book invites you, the reader, to discover the results you can achieve through a more comprehensive and unified approach to the dream process. It gives you advice on how to carry out your own research. Reading this book will help you become better aware of the role played by your body at the meeting point between dreams and reality, between the tangible and the intangible (Chapter 1). The book describes an efficient method for observing the dream process (Chapter 2) and explains the results you can achieve with it through your own experimentation (Chapter 3). Through your personal exploration of the whole dream process you will be able to verify for yourself the reality of certain faculties of the mind which are commonly considered to be "paranormal". You will see that they can be explained rationally. Chapter 4 of the book explains how you can use the dream process to find answers to your questions, whether they regard your daily life (health, work, relationships, life guidance) or your artistic or scientific creativity. The last chapter (Chapter 5) explains why faculties today considered to be paranormal are destined to a natural collective awakening.

With this book, I invite you to observe your dreams and their connections with your reality, with a mind as neutral as possible. Try, then, to forget all you have ever heard about dreams, and just look at them and observe the whole dream process, and not only the dreams. Everything I assert in the book can be verified through personal experience by using the proposed method of observation. With this method everyone, even the most skeptical person, can verify the existence of unusual faculties of the mind, and learn to develop and use them.

Chapter 1: The body at the meeting-point between dreams and reality

1. A body of unexplored ancient knowledge about Man

Ancient legal systems contain one of the most authentic, and least exploited, sources of spiritual knowledge of Man. In ancient civilizations, the modern separation between Economy, Law, Science and what we have come to call "Religion" did not exist. All these fields of knowledge were united. This is why ancient legal systems contain not only legal principles, but also knowledge of nature and of Man. While we tend to limit our attention to the material world, the "primitive" people who invented the ancient legal systems were open to all aspects of life. They explored the material world, the intangible world and the synergies between them. Their approach to Man was comprehensive in a way that ours is not. They considered the human body to be a fundamental link between the tangible and the intangible. Due to their more comprehensive and unified approach to life, they had a better understanding than we do of the way the mind functions, and they applied this knowledge to the legal field. The ancient Romans, for example, used this knowledge to create an efficient legal system. Roman law is the root of many modern legal systems, and is until today studied in many faculties of law. During my own training as a lawyer in France, I had occasion to study the history of law and ancient Roman law. This gave me the idea of applying this ancient body of knowledge to the field of dreams, and led me to widen the scope of observation of the dreaming process. The wisdom of this ancient civilization, transparent in its legal creations, allowed me to become aware that to obtain a better understanding of the dream process, we must observe that process from both a material and an immaterial viewpoint. Therefore, we must consider the dream as an intangible phenomenon occurring in a tangible body. When we observe, through dreams, the connections between the tangible and the intangible, we come to see the preeminent role played by the body in the informational world. This, in turn, leads to unprecedented insight into the functioning of the human mind, both individual and collective.

2. The body as a bridge between the tangible and the intangible

The ancient Romans had understood that the visible and the invisible sides of life are intermingled, and this occurs especially inside the person.[1] They had deduced from this fact, that we can act directly on material things (human body included), while it is impossible to directly exert an action on intangible things (for example a promise, an idea, etc...). In order to act upon intangible things, one must necessarily use matter as an intermediary, and in such a case this matter is the human body. The person was considered to be a bridge between the material and the intangible aspects of life. From this, without entering into details, the existence in the legal procedure of ancient Rome of the *actio in rem* (ritualistic procedure whose aim was to ask the pontiff (priest-judge) to grant an action upon material things, for example if one wanted to get back a stolen material thing) and of the *actio in personam* (ritualistic procedure whose aim was to request from the pontiff an action on people in order to act through them upon the intangible world, for example in the case of a promise, a pontiff has no direct physical power over the intangible promise. He can only order the person who promised to keep the promise or else he will be punished).

Those interested in the ancient Roman law, can read my legal works developing this topic.[2] *In the following pages I apply this ancient procedural knowledge to the dream process. As you will see, this allows to widen considerably the usual scope in which dreams are studied. I am now going to describe, thanks to this ancient procedural knowledge, the role played by the body in the dreaming process.*

3. The body as a transmitter and receiver of information

If we want to understand what a dream is, we have to replace this phenomenon in its natural frame and firstly we have to observe the role played by the body at the meeting point of dream and reality, between the visible and the invisible world. The role played by the body as a bridge between the tangible and the intangible was well known by the ancient Romans, who used it successfully in the legal field. In order to understand the dreaming process, we must go beyond the dream which actually forms only a part of a much wider process. Let us first begin to observe the natural environment in which dreams occur. When observing life upon earth, we can notice the existence of two kinds of reality: what we can call a "material" or a "tangible world" and what we can call an "immaterial" or an "intangible" world. The material world is made of everything we can touch, see, or move, for example a flower, a chair, a boat, a house and also the human body. The intangible world is composed of intangible things, like ideas, emotions, perfumes but also the human mind, which we cannot see or touch. We can schematically represent these observations in the following diagram: (diagram n° 1).

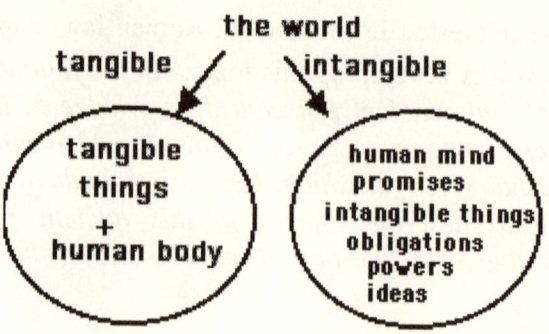

However, this diagram is not fully correct. You have to observe more in depth the real word to see that obviously the material and the immaterial worlds are not disconnected. On the contrary, they overlap and are in constant interaction, and this is particularly true for human beings. We can therefore draw a more exact diagram: (diagram n° 2)

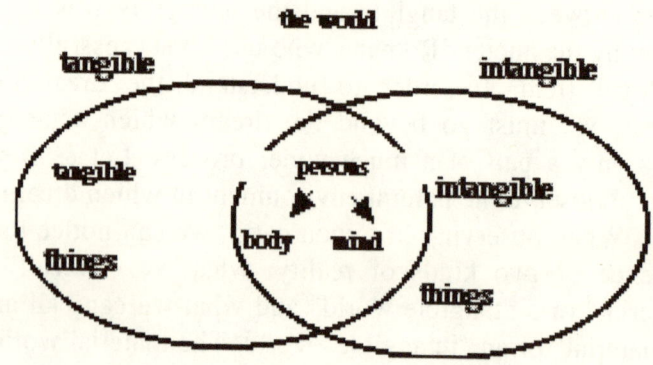

In this diagram we can clearly understand that human beings through their bodies pertain to the material world, while with their minds, thoughts, feelings, emotions, odors and so on, they belong to the intangible world. In other words, human beings appear to be the eternal natural bridge between the tangible and the intangible. Societies, we generally consider to be primitive, did not fail to notice this important aspect of human life. On the contrary, they took this fact into consideration in their philosophy of life. In opposition, our civilization being mainly focused on the material world shows a great ignorance and a great contempt regarding many areas of the intangible world. Sometimes we simply deny the existence of some intangible realities we are unable to explain from a materialist point of view. From this, we learnt very little about the functioning of the intangible world and we ignore, for example, the following fundamental rule that we can find in ancient Roman law:

In order to act upon the intangible world, we always need a tangible means and the human body is an excellent means to reach the intangible. Through the body everyone is a natural bridge between the material and the intangible worlds. In other words, it is impossible to reach directly the intangible. We can do it only through matter, for example through our body.

The ancient Romans knew that it was impossible to act upon the intangible without using a tangible thing. Indeed, in the legal field for example, the only way to act upon an intangible promise, is to act upon tangible people so that they keep their promise. In the same way, it is impossible to directly act upon ideas which are also intangible realities. However, we are able to transmit them through speech thanks to the body and today also thanks to computers. Generally speaking, we deny the reality of all the intangible things (and also of some tangible things) which we are unable to perceive. If, for example, we were unable to sense odors, they would not exist for us. Every person lives in his/her own and/or unique reality composed of all the realities he/she senses and accepts. The reality accepted by the western world is very different from the reality that is accepted by so called primitive tribes. In order to admit the existence of realities we cannot perceive (for example the existence of a foreign country we have never visited), we must trust the people who speak or write about this reality. In this case, though we are unable to perceive them, we admit the existence of certain things. We have accepted that they form part of our own reality. Sometimes, it can be very hard to explain to someone a reality that we know very well, but which does not exist in our interlocutor's world. **In such a case we make use of everything known by this person to help describe this new reality and have it accepted.** Sometimes, it is so difficult to explain the existence of things unknown to other people, that they may think that your discourse is sheer nonsense and consequently uninteresting. This is generally what often happens with dreams. Every night, dreams convey information that our conscious minds are not aware of, because conscious minds are focused on their own reality. Nevertheless, this information exists and is continuously soaked up by our body in the immediate or in the remote environment. **Dreams are a means to access an important source of information that the conscious mind, in our state of mental development, is unable to perceive.** The actual perceptive potential of the human beings clearly appears through a broader and comprehensive approach to the dreaming process, **that is to say, an approach not confined to dreams and to their interpretation. Such an approach considers that dreams are the result of an exchange process.** In fact, dreams appear to be the result of a kind of "continuous breathing" between the inner and outer worlds of individuals. When we breath we take air in, we transform it and reject it. Through breathing we are continuously operating some exchanges with our environment through our lungs and also through the whole surface of the skin. This air contains a lot of intangible things and has a lot of properties. For example, it can be warm and our skin transmits the information "it's warm". This is a reception of information from the intangible environment. Regarding the emission of information, our body emits in the air its own heat, its odors, its hormones, its energy, its emotions and its electromagnetic field. Ideas and thoughts are also emitted in the environment through the body, whether or not we use speech to do so. We can schematically represent as follows a human being surrounded by all he/she emits in the atmosphere and which contains the energy field that many spiritual traditions have acknowledged and called the "aura": Diagram n° 3 a person in an *information sphere*

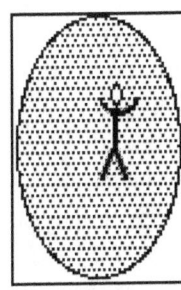

The information sphere includes any invisible information emitted by a person + invisible information from the place where the person is standing.
=
The atmosphere surrounding a person

Millenniums ago, the inner human energy fields were well known by Chinese medicine. The aim of Chinese acupuncture is to allow a correct flow of energy in the body in order to keep it healthy or to restore good health. Since 1875, the western world has discovered that the brain contains electric currents. And since 1929, we have been technologically able to observe the electrical emissions of the brain thanks to the electroencephalograph. This device permits to amplify the electric signals which are picked up by electrodes fixed on people's skulls.[3] A researcher called Kirlian has also invented in 1939 a technology that enables to photograph the energy field of human beings and of plants.[4] Our body is surrounded with invisible emanations, which are real even although they are invisible. Some of these emanations, like the electricity emitted by the brain can now be scientifically measured. From now we shall call these emanations surrounding every person, an *information sphere*. Although we are unable to consciously perceive this *information sphere*, we consider it to be the special ambiance of a person, the one which we perceive on the first meeting with a person.[5] This *information sphere* contains also much information coming from the environment where the body of the person stands. This last information can be constituted by emanations of some other people, the emissions of plants and of animals, also by solar or earth energy. It is always through the body that you can access the intangible information world as emitters and as receivers of information. For example, when you speak, you emit sound information with your tongue. You receive sound information from the environment (mainly) with your ears. In the case of sound, this information is clear for your conscious mind which accepts it, and from that, you admit the reality of sounds, even though they are invisible. The same occurs with regards to odors whose reality we admit even though we cannot touch or see them. Everyone emits a lot of information into the environment, such as: emotions, feelings, odors, noises, thoughts.[6] Continuous breathing occurs between the information received by the body and the information it emits in the environment. We permanently exchange information at different levels. But our conscious mind makes strict selections out of this mass of information that our body is able to receive from the environment.[7] Such a drastic selection deprives us of a huge wealth of information and, this selection is probably due to the fact that we use only a small portion of the capabilities of the brain. Many people know from experience that the content of dreams can be directly influenced by previous daily life events. For example, the characters of a movie can appear in your dreams mixed with some personal elements. Daily life concerns and problems also appear in dreams. A human being cannot survive without a permanent exchange with its environment. **Dreams, like the majority of physical and psychological processes, consist mainly in an** emission/reception of information. **Dreams are information emitted through the body and are in relation with the information the body has received from its environment.** Some information that dreams convey to the conscious mind are clear, but the majority of dream information appears like nonsense to the conscious mind. Sometimes, the dream content appears grotesque, ridiculous or threatening. As we generally do not understand the meaning of dreams and as we do not know why dreams exist, we simply tend to reject them. We do not pay the attention we should pay to them, because we consider they are useless. This attitude constitutes a fundamental mistake of modern world which has not been able to take profit from this natural ability, to develop itself on a material as well as on a spiritual ground. If we were able to understand the dream language, we would be also able to access a wider range of information and we would, in doing so, go beyond the limits in which our conscious mind confines us.[8] Taking all this into account, more than 13 years ago I began exploring the dream process through the perspective of the *third choice*. That is to say, that I admitted the existence of a material world and of an intangible world and that I tried to better understand their connections and their synergies through the observation of the dreaming process. Taking into account the fact that the dreaming process is always linked to the real environment of dreams, I have proceeded to a systematic observation of the connection between the information conveyed by my dreams and the information existing in my real environment. This method of work has been very fruitful. I have learned a lot, but overall I can now foresee the potential of development of the human intelligence, and of its vast and unbelievable capabilities. Of course, you do not need to believe me. Just make your own experience and check everything for yourself, I shall tell you how you can do it. Through my experience, I have noticed that dreams act as a bridge between the conscious mind, and a much wider consciousness, from now on the *greater consciousness*. The *greater consciousness* contains much more information than the *conscious mind*. It particularly contains all the information that the body picks up in its environment (immediate or remote) and within itself and that does not reach the conscious mind, as we are not yet enough developed for that. We can schematically represent as follows the situation of people who almost "do not dream" and who do not pay attention to their dreams. These persons benefit very little from the information picked up by the body which transmits it to the *greater consciousness*, which in turn conveys it in part to the *conscious mind* through dreams. Which can be schematized as follows: Diagram n° 4.

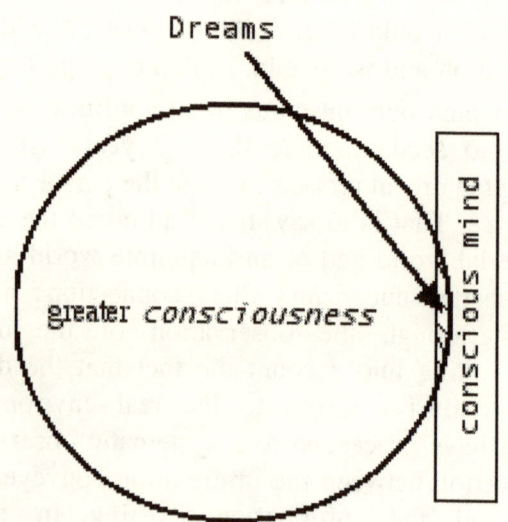

By investigating the dream process through the angle of the understanding of the connection between dreams and reality, it is possible to attain the following state of development. In this state, the *conscious mind* has been progressively enlarged and we can profit better from the information contained in the *greater consciousness*. In

other words, the *conscious mind* grows, while by understanding the dream language it has become possible to take better advantage of the information picked up by the body, not recognized by the conscious mind, but nevertheless received by the *greater consciousness*. Which can be schematized as follows:
Diagram n° 5

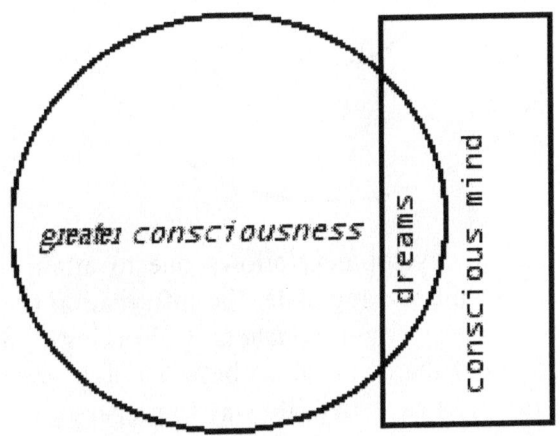

A third stage of development is much more interesting than the previous ones. It can be schematized as follows:

(diagram 6).

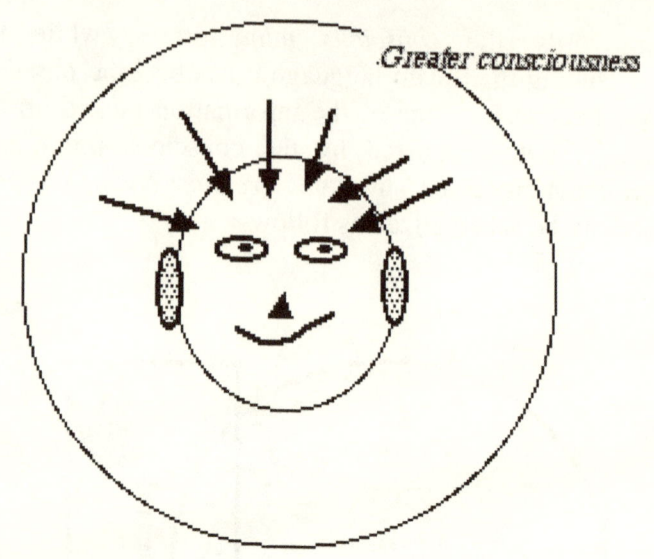

This stage of development allows one to attain directly and to use in the waking state, the information contained in the *greater consciousness*. Working on the investigation of the connections between your dreams and your reality is an easy and safe way to prepare yourself for this stage of development. People having achieved this stage have developed capabilities that are generally considered to be "paranormal", magic or simply unbelievable. But, in fact these capacities are the potential that future humanity as a whole should develop, provided the *third choice* is made. Disappeared civilizations had already developed these capabilities long before us. Again, you do not need to believe me, just verify it for yourself. In order to make your own experiment, I am going to give you the information you need for a successful experience, in the next chapter. Through your own work on the connection between your dreams and your reality, you will realize the reality of capacities like: telepathy, prediction of the future, knowledge of remote events etc... As the author Robert Moss also stated, all these dormant capacities "come richly alive in dreams".[9] Then, just do your own experiments!

Chapter 2: How to observe the connections between your dreams and your reality

In this Chapter, I am going to explain how to efficiently observe your dream process in order to get the valuable results I shall describe later on, and also many other results that you will discover on your own.

1. How to observe your dreaming process

The best way to observe the dreaming process is not to focus on dreams. On the contrary, observe simultaneously your dreams and your reality. Write down your dreams and the main events of your waking life, and carry on simple experiments in real life in order to observe their consequences on the dreaming process. If it is true that reality influences dreams,[10] you will discover very soon for yourself how much your dreams shape your reality, even when you forget them. A continuous exchange of information takes place between us and the environment. We are conscious of some of these exchanges, but unconscious of the majority of them. A great amount of information on the immaterial world that surrounds us is picked up by our body without entering our conscious mind. This information is nevertheless stored in the *greater consciousness* and dreams are one of the means to access it, provided we are able to decipher our own dream language. At first sight some dreams seem to have no connection with reality and so, unimportant. Through keeping a dream-reality journal you will gradually see the connection which exists between the dreaming process and the information world in which you live. The existence of such a connection will allow you to understand very precisely the meaning of your own and unique dream language. In this field, everyone has his own dream vocabulary, and personal work is absolutely necessary if you want to understand your dreams and take a benefit from them. For this work you cannot expect help from ancient or modern dream dictionaries which pretend to give you a ready to use interpretation of dream symbols. It is better to avoid this kind of literature which frequently leads to mistranslation of your unique dream vocabulary. Moreover, this kind of literature is full of fears and superstitions passed from generation to generation. It is regrettable that dream dictionaries are easily accessible literature and contribute to discredit dream messages and make more difficult the understanding of the dreaming process. Every person has a unique dream language, this cannot be stressed enough. However one can share with some nuances, some great dream symbols common to human groups or to the whole humanity. For example, for many dreamers the symbol "house" can stand for the body, the symbol "on the left" is for the female aspect of the mind and the symbol "on the right" for the male aspect. What is "in the forefront" relates to the future for many dreamers, while what is "behind" generally relates to the past of the dreamer. Streets, highways, country roads, lanes, or mountain tracks are varied representations of destiny. These symbols appear in dreams when you have to make some important decisions regarding your future. At the beginning of your observation work, you can efficiently help yourself with dictionaries of symbols, which do not relate to dreams but explain the meaning of symbols throughout the ages and for different people.[11] An interest in the meaning of symbols is an excellent way to make your brain more flexible in order to better understand your own world of symbols. We need mental flexibility mainly to understand a reality directly out of reach, but conveyed to our conscious mind by dreams. The best and easiest way I have found to discover the meaning of my dreams and to access more information on my intangible environment is keeping a dream-reality journal in which I write down all the dreams I remember, the main lines of my reality, and the experiments I did. For example, as an experiment you can decide to sleep in special places, go on a diet, overeat, visit many people or completely isolate yourself for some time while continuing to keep your dream-reality journal.[12] I have experienced all the above, and as a result I have detected the important things to write down regarding dreams and reality. My experience can save your time, though everyone can use the "dream-reality" method for a specific aim.

2. How to record your dreams

It is much easier to remember your dreams when you wake up, this is therefore the best time to write them down. Some authors also advise to make note of them during the night and therefore to have everything ready at hand e.g.; paper and pencils. It can be done, but paying so much attention to dreams can be stressful and sometimes blocking. If you want to do a long-drawn-out job, then do it in a relaxed way, sleep normally. With practice, the memory of dreams improves and one of the ways to improve your memory is to trust it. If at the beginning you cannot remember your dreams do not be discouraged. Everybody dreams and it is very easy to reactivate this kind of memory. If this is your case, please see the frequently asked questions at the end of this book.[13] At the beginning, the fundamental attitude is to be neutral and to observe the dreaming process. Do not try to understand all your dreams at first. Simply write down all you remember and above all, avoid complex analysis of dream messages. In time you will be able to understand precisely your own dream symbols. You will also notice that some dreams are crystal-clear and do not need to be interpreted through a psychoanalytical approach or another method. A second fundamental attitude to be adopted is to have the courage to write down everything you remember even if these memories are painful, shameful, scary or disturbing. Be neutral like a movie-camera and tolerant. Write down all you can remember. **All the dreams you can remember must be written down without selecting the ones you believe to be important**. Every dream is important if you want to understand the connection between your dreams and your reality. For example, a short and simple dream like "I have dreamt that some beautiful shoes were on sale at the butchers" contains valuable information. Also do not be afraid to take note of things regarding death or death itself. Most of the time death announces a big change in your life or personality or a rebirth. You will see that aspects of your own personality are often represented by people you know. Regarding your own death, why being afraid of dreams announcing it? Why not pay attention to them as they can also be warning dreams that can save your life? Through your dreams you can be reassured about life, because you can observe that dreams always prepare your immediate and remote future. Therefore, dreams are an indication that your life is not about to come to an end. In dream literature, many cases of dreams relating to actual death have been quoted. They show that the event is announced in the dreaming state.[14] Dreams prepare us to leave this life in peace, when the moment comes and help us avoid being permanently and uselessly afraid of dying. This is very useful in the present world of terrorism. When our own death approaches, dreams inform us. They prepare us for the passage or on the contrary they warn us about a danger that can be avoided.[15] Having spoken of the hard subject of death, let us now speak about life. In the dreaming state, regardless of sex and age, everybody can give birth or be pregnant. It is no longer the female's privilege. Most of the time, being pregnant and giving birth are related to creativity. As for sexual dreams, they can simply convey a non-sexual message and you should not hesitate to note each detail. For example, dreaming about an interrupted intercourse does not necessarily mean that this will happen in reality or that it is a sexual message. It can for example mean a sudden, unexpected and unpleasant end of a relationship with a relative. As for bananas, doors, staircases, birds and other symbols that Freud considered to be sexual symbols, one should update ones ideas. Sexuality has become freer than During Freud's time, and consequently dreams and reality have changed a lot in this respect. In short, we should take note of all the dreams in the way they speak to our memory, describe the dream characters and the stage of the dream in a manner as accurate and detailed as possible. For example if you dream of a cat, you should take note of its color, its size, its spatial position in comparison with yours or with the spatial position of other dream characters (to the left, to the right, behind, in front of, in the middle, etc..). You should also take note of everything you perceive about this cat. Take note of the appearance of its fur, and of its eyes. Look at both eyes, are-they similar in color? in shape? in their expression? Is it a female or a male cat? From experience, I know that in my dream language, cats represent the souls of the people around me and also my soul. And I know that a cat with an unhealthy fur is related to a person having little physical energy and poor health, that is to say a low level of life-energy. It is of paramount importance to write down all your feelings, even when they seem unrelated with the main topic of the dream. For example, in a dream you can laugh a lot for something that would be horrible and on the contrary you can feel a lot of pain for something that would be insignificant in the waking state. You should write down all your feelings: joy, pain, love, hatred, fear, anger, anxiety, sadness, etc... Also take note of all your physical sensations like: cold, heat, paralysis, lightness, quickness, slowness. If you hear some music in your dream describe it, take note of the content of songs, take also note of the tales you hear, of the characters. You will see that in the dreaming state more communication generally occurs than in reality. In dreams everything is able to speak, from stones to plants and animals. They can speak your own language or some other language. Sometimes, you or other characters can speak some language or only words of some language you do not speak in the waking state. In my dreams, I could notice that when there is a repetition of the same words, sentences or images, this is for important information. Sometimes I can dream of some foreign words whose meaning I do not know and I find it amusing and often instructive to check, when possible, their meaning in a dictionary when I wake up. When I was living in New York, at the limit of Little Italy and China Town, many times I dreamed in Chinese, which language I do not practice but was the dominant language of my close environment. On this ground, there is a lot to understand regarding the learning process of languages. Regarding dreams, it is important to take note of your position in the space when you appear as one of your dream characters. Are you in the center, to the right, to the left, in front of or behind someone, something or a place? Are you standing on the ground, on water or in the sky? You should write down all you remember. For example, all the details of clothes: color, composition and shape, are a great source of valuable dream information. Take also note of all your physical sensations and discomforts: like tooth ache, ear ache, lightness or difficulty of movement, for example because you are carrying a heavy load. You should describe with as much detail as possible everything you carry in the dream state. If it is a luggage, write about its shape, color, weight, easiness or difficulty to carry it, if there are rollers or even wings on your luggage. Do you like your luggage? Did somebody help you to carry it, or did you decide to abandon it because you were carrying useless things, or carrying nothing at all? With which hand did you hold your luggage: right or left hand? Is your luggage in front of you or behind you? Did you push your luggage with difficulty, or was it following you easily? Detailed description is useful, especially at the beginning of your dream-reality work. If you dream about a house, do not hesitate to take note of all the details of this house, even if it takes a long time. The time spent will be greatly rewarded. Describe all the rooms you enter and particularly basement rooms, attics, kitchens and bathrooms. In houses, everything is interesting and informative. From my own experience, I know that the houses of my dreams (when there are not real houses that I "visit" in the dream state), give me accurate information about my health, most of the time. And I could notice, like doctors in antiquity already did it,[16] that physical disorders appear in dreams long before they manifest themselves in reality. Because of this, it is very interesting to get to the meaning of your dreams in order to take preventive action as soon as possible. From my experience, I know for example that the toilets of my dreams are related to the state of my bowels in reality. I know that a water leak in the bathroom of my dreams is connected to fatigue in my waking life. When I write a book, if I dream I see lot of disordered attics, I know my work is messy and should be clarified. But I have a place in my dream houses that I love very much, it is the cellar. It is related to my physical and psychological heritage. I like to visit this room in my dreams, there I find a trap door and when I open it a stone staircase appears. When I am not afraid, I can enter ancient worlds. You will discover by yourself how much you can learn about your body and your mind through the simultaneous observation of dreams and reality. It is also possible to observe how the repetition of real problems reacts on your physical health and to discover why some part of your body will be affected by some kinds of problems. This will allow you to better communicate with your body. Sometimes your body can manifest psychological discomfort before you consciously become aware of it. Another very interesting aspect of dream is nature and its representation. Dreams are very rich in their knowledge of nature. Nature appears in almost all dreams. The symbols, shared with some nuances by the whole humanity, come from nature. In your Dreams you can see stars, moons, suns, oceans, light, obscurity and so on. From experience, I know that when there is wind in my dreams there will be an acceleration of events in my life. When the weather of my dreams is extremely cold, this is for cold people around me in real life, that are extremely selfish. In dreams some people can be represented as plants, and therefore it is very important to describe the plants you can see in your dreams. For example some plants can grow fast and invade all your house. Some other plants have big roots you can see because they have no earth. You can find withered plants or healthy plants with flowers and fruits. Some plants can ask you for some water, a lot of water or only a little. Water is another natural element very common and important in dreams. It is very interesting and useful to know the meaning of the different kinds of water you can see in your dreams like: glass of water, bottle of water, pot of water, bath, shower, river, lake, ocean, rain, swimming pool, wells or puddles. Dreams containing information on water are usually very practical for real life. For example, I could notice through my dream-reality work that when I am offered a glass of crystal-clear water, this announces new good friends in real life. While the message conveyed is very different if the water in the glass is for example dirty or cloudy. I also know from my experience that the sea stands for my *greater consciousness*, or the collective consciousness and that a swimming pool represent the narrowness of modern social life in comparison to the possibilities offered by an unlimited consciousness. Before finishing with the theme of water, I would like to stress again how important it is to take note of all the details of water, as water is as important in dreams as it is in reality. Another important dream symbol is related to destiny. In modern times where people are faced with more and more unstable professional as well as family life, dreams of "roads" are a major theme. And it is interesting to understand them as this kind of dream is of great help to make future decisions. The "road" of your dreams can be a path in a breathtaking natural site or in a dry desert. It can be a jammed highway, or an empty street. You can find yourself in a dream hesitating which way to follow at crossroads or dreams can picture you going round and round the same place. Sometimes you do not know where you are going. While you are in total obscurity you can be helped by a passer by who owns a lamp which sheds light in you path. Dreams of "roads"[17], provided you can understand them, convey important information on your destiny. However this kind of information can also be conveyed by some other dream symbols. For example, although he was very rational, the French philosopher Descartes paid attention to his dreams and made the following one about his destiny while he was writing the Discourse of the Method. This dream was reported by Baillet, as DESCARTES' dreams of November 10, 1619.[18]

> "A short time later, he had a third dream. He dreamt that he found a book on his table without knowing where it came from. He opened it and as he realized that it was a dictionary he became very pleased and thought that this book should be very useful. At the same time he found another book in his hands, which one was also completely new and he did not know where it came from. He saw that this book was a book of poetry from several authors, entitled "corpus poëtarum" etc.. He felt very interested in reading something in this book, opened it and fell on the following line of poetry: "quod

vitae sectabor iter?" (Which way shall I follow in my life?)."

The other reported dreams gave some guidance to Descartes. Notably, they pointed out a strong disequilibrium between the right and the left sides of his dream-body. Which could perhaps mean a prevalence of one of his (masculine or feminine) element over the other during his waking life. But this is only a suggestion because René Descartes never kept a dream-reality diary and we have not enough dream-reality material about him.

When you dream about "roads" it is important to describe all you see and all you do. For example, if you are driving a car, you should note if the steering wheel is on the left or on the right, if somebody else is driving your car, the way you drive your car, and if it is during the night, with or without headlights or during the day. Is driving easy or not? Making the connection of these kinds of dreams with what happens in your waking life is a mine of useful information to find the right way to follow in an unstable environment. We can benefit greatly from these dreams especially when pursuing a professional career or for making business decisions.

To summarize, it is crucial to write down everything you remember from your dreams and also to take note of all the dreams without making a selection within them. At the beginning, the best is not to try to immediately understand your dream language, it is better to simply observe what happens and to take note of it, as if you were a neutral reporter. An author could advise that when telling your dream you should explain everything as if you were telling them to an extra-terrestrial being (Gale Delaney). In fact, the "translation" of your dream language will be made easier after some time, because, as you will see: the same dream symbols always appear in connection with the same waking life situation.[19] And this can be noticed only after a certain time. At the beginning of my research, I made for example the following mistake: whenever I dreamt that my mother had won the lottery, I called her to check if my dream was "real". But through my observation of the connection between my dreams and my reality, I now know that when I have this dream this means an unexpected income for myself. There was another mistake I made at the beginning, that many people working on their dreams tend to do: I tried to understand all my dreams on a psychological angle using Jung or Freud's theories. Most of the time, I was misled by these theories. Instead, the meaning of my dreams would have been made simple, very clear and direct through the dream-reality work during a period of time long enough. Now, I have become able to make a better use of psychoanalytical modern method of dream interpretation for some of my dreams, but not the majority of them, which I can now by experience determine as "psychological symbolic dreams". I could observe that in my case, these kinds of dreams occur in some well determined circumstances. Gale Delaney,[20] an American psychoanalyst, specialized in dream interpretation proposes today a psychological approach of dream interpretation, much more open than the ones proposed in their times by Jung or Freud. In her book *All About Dreams*, after having summarized the evolution of ideas in this field, she proposes her method, the "interview" method. This method makes more room to the dreamer than to the interpreters and their theories. In doing so, the author corrects the mistake that, in her opinion, was made by her predecessors who were too authoritative in the field of dream interpretation.[21] In Gale Delaney's opinion, the main role of the dream therapist is to ask the dreamer the right questions during the interview so that he/she can express the content and understand the meaning of his/her dream. All of us have unresolved psychological problems, this is life. Dreams are an opportunity to point at these problems often rejected by the conscious mind, and to foresee the way to overcome them and feel better. I have observed that the most important psychological dreams appear, when they are reactivated by a waking life event, but also when I have the energy and the peace of mind to work them. This is why they generally happen when one makes a retreat, and this even if no external events reactivate them. In such a case I feel that the energy I do not use for outer life is used for inner repairing. The more psychological problems you can solve, the more your dream capabilities will be available for some other tasks. After more than 13 years of work on my dreams, a small portion of them -that I am now able to detect easily from the other kinds of dreams- need a psychological approach. Whereas, the wide majority of my dreams are understandable more accurately through the simultaneous observation of dream and reality over a long period of time. Therefore be patient, take note of every dream and don't forget to observe also your reality. The time you will spend on that will be widely rewarded by all the time you will win and all the bad things and mistakes you will be able to avoid, thanks to the understanding of the information conveyed by your dreams. Now, let us see how to take note of your reality.

3. *How to take notes about your waking life*

When you take note of your reality, you do not need to be as precise as with dreams. You only need to outline the main events of the day. Some observations are very important in order to understand the way you pick up information from your environment. For example, it is useful to note the places where you have been during the day, the places where you have slept, and above all the people you have met. Regarding these people, just write down the main subject of your conversation and the circumstances of your encounter, for example: planned meeting or mere coincidence. It is also important to note your feelings (joy, sadness, indifference etc...) or sensations (well-being, fatigue, nervousness, anxiety, boredom) and to note the location where the meeting took place. Locations are very important elements, insofar as every place is full of intangible information that the body can pick up.[22] The body also picks up all the intangible information which emanates from a person or comes from a group of people. Everybody has already sensed the different atmospheres of places like a church, a pub, a library, a forest, or a beach. It is also easy to perceive the difference in atmosphere between your home and other people's home. The atmosphere we are speaking of is not the one created by physical decoration but by intangible information contained in the house. In fact we are able to sense the varying energies of different premises. Some people have poor consciousness of these differences, while others are highly sensitive to this difference. But, even though one cannot consciously perceive the intangible energy of a place, one's *greater consciousness*, nevertheless, stores all the intangible information of the places where the body has been. Through dreams one can access this information. People who are very rational, and therefore closed to this kind of perception, can take advantage of the dream-reality work and this will counterbalance their lack of conscious perception. In order to make use of dreams, you should write down all the main events of your waking life: daily activities, trips, parties, moving, big decisions you make, and important achievements. Those engaged in a creative task should also note the different stages of their work and the way they live their creativity (for example: the days when they feel happy and satisfied, and the days when they hesitate, feel discontent and uninspired). If you would like to use your dreams to improve your physical and mental health, to detect future health problems,[23] it is important to take note of all that regards your health in waking, life even the light discomforts you experience. Regarding physical health: you can for example take note of a cold, a flue, muscular tensions, good or bad physical condition. If you are an athlete take note of your training progresses. Regarding mental health: take note of your good or bad moods when you wake up, during the day, after meetings or when you go to unusual places. All this information is very useful. Time and patience are required, but the results are worthwhile. One of the results I believe to be most interesting is to know that dreams act as health scanners. They show what is wrong and what is going to be wrong if we do not take appropriate preventive action. I shall speak more in depth on this topic later, because it is one of the fields where simultaneous observation of dreams and reality opens the horizons of understanding (of health, illnesses, and healing). For now, let us see some of the results of my observation of the dream process.

Chapter 3: Some of the results achieved thanks to this method of observation

Through this approach to dreams, I have learnt a lot about myself, other people, animals and nature. There is still much to be discovered, and I continue my research. What's more, I have developed new abilities and my intuition has improved considerably. In addition, I feel more at peace and trustful because I can better see through my dreams what my immediate future will be. Everyone can make his/her own discoveries according to his/her own interests. As a lawyer, I am particularly interested in the links between people, in the functioning of groups, and in the organization of societies. Consequently I have used this dream-reality work to better understand what happens on an intangible level between people. This was of great interest to the first "priest-lawyers" of ancient worlds, like the Roman pontiffs we already mentioned, or the ancient Egyptians. The following are my discoveries.

1. Understanding energy exchanges between people and with the environment

As I have already explained, everyone emits all types of information through the body and receives through the whole body information which comes from other people and places. Everyone is surrounded by his/her own unique ambiance which we call *information sphere*. In this *information sphere,* the information we emit is mixed with the information we receive from the people around us or from the place where we are located. We can

schematically represent this fact as follows:
Diagram n° 7

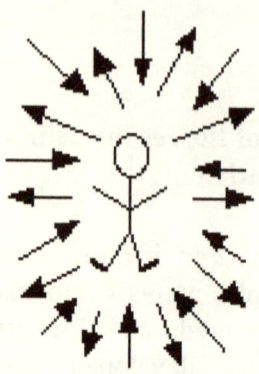

When you stand beside another person, your *information sphere* mixes with the *information sphere* of the other person. For this reason, your body picks up much more information on people than your conscious mind. What happens when two people meet can be represented as follows.
Diagram n° 8

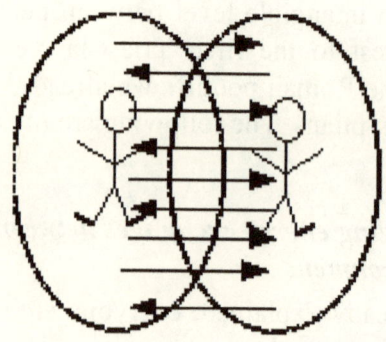

When two people meet, an intense exchange occurs between their *information spheres*. While the conscious mind receives direct information like: speech, odors, visual information, the whole body picks up all the intangible messages which emanate from the person and the place of the meeting. The body, as a whole is able to pick up intangible information like: feelings, thoughts, the physical and mental energy of the other person and also information about where this person lives, his/her family context, his/her her background and so on... An actual scanning of the personality and of the body occurs, through which the *greater consciousness* knows everything about your human and material environment. Through the body, the *greater consciousness* receives much more information than the conscious mind. You can verify this yourself through your dream-reality journal. All the information received goes to the *greater consciousness,* some of it can reach the *conscious mind* through dreams, and some goes directly to the conscious mind through what we call intuition or clairvoyance. Dreams allow us to access additional information on the people we meet. This can help us detect the real intentions of people who say fine words but have bad intentions. Even if the conscious mind was seduced by their words, if we call on our dreams, understand them and accept them, our dreams always show people as they really are (and ourselves too). The body, contrary to the conscious mind, is not subjected to preconceived cultural standards. The body is very natural, it picks up all the information in its environment, whatever the language spoken. However, at the beginning of the dream-reality work, you should be very careful, because you will need some time to be able to tell the difference between the characters in your dreams that stand for you and the ones that actually represent other people. You will notice that many characters represent you, your qualities and your defects.[24] It is very tempting to credit only other people with unpleasant qualities. It is therefore important not to judge others too quickly. Do not use dreams only to judge. You should also use your conscious mind and compare your "dream-feeling" with reality. In addition, as you gradually perceive more and more information about people, good and bad information, you will need to be more and more tolerant and continue loving people despite the many defects you detect in them. No one is perfect. In time, dream-reality work will allow you to distinguish between characters standing for you and characters actually standing for other people. A simple and interesting experiment can be done in this field after you have worked some time on observing the connections between your dreams and your reality. This experiment consists in completely isolating yourself at least for a few days.[25] Isolation "cleans" your *information sphere* of the emanations from people who are usually around you. After this isolation you will be better able to tell the difference between your own atmosphere and the atmospheres of others. You will better sense the *information spheres* of others to which you will become much more sensitive. I have done this experiment several times, for different reasons. During it, I have tested the "Crab Apple" remedy invented by the British Doctor Bach which aids mental and physical purification.[26] If you do this experiment, you will be able to understand why ancient people were so interested in rites of physical and psychological purification and also the practice of dream incubation which I will discuss later. On another level, you will also be able to see for yourself that some dreams cannot be explained in relation to you. Indeed, it is as if these dreams pertained to other people, as if you were dreaming for someone else. Such phenomena often occur in couples where intense and continuous exchange between *information spheres* occurs through day to day living. The author Isabel Allende also noticed this phenomenon occurring between herself and her husband. She writes: "Our bond is so strong that our dreams are intermingled..."[27]

A highly sensitive person may have recurring nightmares while his/her companion, for example, recently traumatized by a car crash sleeps peacefully. In the same way, when we travel, our dreams contain information from the new places where we are sleeping and from the people who have slept there before. We need some time to fill a room with our own *information sphere* and the first day in a hotel you can dream things that are related to the other people who have slept there before.[28] This allows us to understand why so many spiritual traditions have rites and techniques to purify physical surroundings. Often when you travel, part of your dreams is not related to you. It is therefore useless to try to interpret them with one of the dream interpretation methods. You would only waste your time. Through the dream-reality experience, you can also see the role you and others play in the formation of a collective atmosphere. For example, you may feel happy in one village and sense an unpleasant atmosphere or become anxious in another. This difference is not just a coincidence, the two different atmospheres were created by the emanations of the people (past and present) of the villages, mixed with the energy of the place. It is up to you to make your own deductions and to experiment to tell the difference between psychically polluted and unpolluted places. Though most human beings do not pay attention to energy pollution, this pollution affects them at different levels. Energy pollution caused by places or people can undermine your energy and contribute to create bad moods and anxiety, otherwise unexplainable. (You can feel for example very sad in a beautiful palace). On the other hand a good psychic atmosphere contributes to inner well-being and increases creativity. It is not mere coincidence that some places have always inspired creativity. One day we shall certainly be able to measure the psychic energy of places and the inner energy of people. In the meantime, one can easily notice that when artists begin to settle in the worst parts of town (because rent is cheap), the atmosphere of those places slowly changes. Soon it costs so much to live there, that artists cannot afford it and they move to other parts of town.[29]

Those whose sensitivity to this kind of energy is dormant can greatly benefit from their dreams to compensate for their lack of sensitivity in the waking state. However, the more you do the dream-reality work, the more sensitive you become.[30] Thanks to my dream-reality work I have become more sensitive to my environment and I have also experienced distance communication. I could observe that I can pick up at a distance everything that is of interest to me or that is on the same energy wave length. I have also noticed that distance communication during dreams or during the waking state is much easier when there is a strong bond between people. Therefore distance communication is made easier between members of the same family, between lovers, and between mothers and their young children, as this is one of the strongest human bonds. The author Nina Berberova affirmed she picked up, through a dream, information on the circumstances of her parents' death.[31] There is much to discover for yourself regarding the invisible connections between people and how they function. Finally, I would like to speak about an interesting practical application in this field: making appointments. I have often noticed that when, in the dream state, I make an appointment to meet someone in real life, I always meet this person as we say "by coincidence". Moreover I have noticed that the appointments accepted during the dream state were never missed, even in the most unexpected or difficult circumstances. For example, in one dream I had made an appointment with a good friend of mine. In the waking life, I was very sad to have lost touch with him because we had been unable to exchange addresses after moving. All I knew was that he had moved to Morocco, his home country. Upon awakening from this dream I had the irresistible urge to go to the Champs Elysées. Though I hate going to this crowded and noisy part of Paris, upon awakening, I followed my urge and went there by the metro. When I arrived at the station, just as I was about to use one of the escalators to exit, I do not know why, but a stranger prevented me from doing so. I used another escalator instead and, when I arrived at the top, I was surprised and delighted to find my friend before me, walking amongst a crowd of people on this large Paris avenue. He was also very pleased to see me as he was in Paris for just a few days and had unsuccessfully tried to find me through the telephone company. Needless to say, that this aspect of dreams is of great practical and philosophical interest. This now leads us to the question of space and time in dreams.

2. A different approach to space-time

The concepts of space and time exist in the dream world, though they do not follow the same laws as they do in waking life. When studying dreams, it is difficult to know when space and time pertain to the intangible world of dreams or when dreams are simply permeated with the laws of space and time of the real world. In fact the two different sets of laws are usually intermingled in the dream world. Therefore, it is difficult to explain the space-time concept in dreams, but I will do my best to explain what I have discovered about this subject through my dream-reality work.

a) The concept of space in dreams

Through dream-reality work, you can see how much your dreams are permeated by information from the real world. You can also see that sometimes dreams contain information coming from remote places. Our bodies are able to receive information coming from people who can be very far from us, for example, in a foreign country. Here the laws of physical space do not apply. They are replaced by a different set of laws, including laws of attraction, laws of energy, laws of thought, laws of feelings, etc. When, for example, we receive information about people who are far from us in physical space, these people are in reality very close to us in a different way. This proximity is due not to space proximity but to proximity in the fields of love, energy, and thinking. The body is able to receive thoughts emitted by people wherever they are located in the physical space. You will be able to verify this fact very easily through dream-reality work. You can also find an abundance of testimony on this possibility in literature. For example, the writer Nina Berberova asserts in her biography that in a dream she was able to perceive information about her parents who had remained in Russia when she moved to France. In fact, our body is able to perceive remote information and remote events that are of interest to us. Dreams not only allow us to overcome the material laws of space, they also allow us to overcome the physical laws of time.

b) The concept of time in dreams
Again, it is difficult in dreams to distinguish what refers to dream time from what refers to "physical" time, for these two concepts of time are intermingled in the dream state. Through dream-reality work, you will see that your dreams convey information on the present, on the past, and on your immediate or remote future. I am now going to explain why we have access in dreams to information regarding the past and the future.

The past in dreams:
Through your own dream-reality work, you will see that some dreams convey information on past events that you were not aware of in reality. In such cases, what seems to be happening is that your greater consciousness was informed of the event when it took place, and then held on to the information, to which the conscious mind had access only two weeks later through a dream. You will see through dream-reality work that we can obtain access to information from a remote past, for example information

on our ancestors and other people who died a long time ago. In such cases, perhaps we have access to a memory stored in our body, which contains information from all the people who contributed to its formation. Through dream-reality work, it is also easy to see that we have access to a rich collective consciousness, from which we may glean information on the past, present or future of humanity.

The future in dreams

Since our *conscious mind* is subjected to the space-time rules of the tangible world, it is much more difficult to accept a "memory" of the future. In consequence, foretelling the future seems impossible, unbelievable, paranormal or miraculous. But you can see for yourself, as some people already have, that dreaming your future is something very common and trivial.[32] You will notice that you can dream even unimportant future events. In fact, every night we dream our immediate and sometimes remote future, I believe this is due to the fact that life does not work the way we believe. In fact, it is as if life were lived in reverse: every night in the dream state we program ourselves for the waking state. Everything happens as if real life was an acting out of the role chosen and prepared by the *greater consciousness* and conveyed particularly through dreams to the *conscious mind*. That is to say that sleep is the time when we (the *greater consciousness*) program the events of our waking life. From this, it is easy to explain that dreams foretell the future because this future is put in place by the *greater consciousness*. We can compare this to the way you foretell, in waking life, that you will do a special thing, on next Saturday let's say, because you have scheduled it. The difference between the dream-state and the waking state "in foretelling the future" is that far more information from the *greater consciousness* is available in the dream state than in the waking state. Therefore the *greater consciousness* plans the future more accurately. Very few people are aware of this. Most of us believe that the conscious mind plays the main role in handling our waking lives. If you pay attention to your dreams, you will notice some exceptional occurrences of dreams foretelling the future. If however, you do the dream-reality work, you will gain a better understanding of your dream vocabulary. You will come to the conclusion that precognitive dreams are banal, and you will begin to take advantage of this phenomenon. Fortunately, throughout history, some people have had crystal clear prophetic dreams, so human beings know that dreams can show the future. This was the main aspect that interested the people of antiquity and which prevented them from studying the dreaming process more in depth. Today premonitory dreams are still considered wonderful, paranormal or divine, that is when they are not simply denied. However, through dream-reality work you will see for yourself that your brain has the natural ability to tell the future, and that like all other abilities it can be developed. The writer Isabel Allende who pays attention to her dreams has asserted that, thanks to dreams she was able to foretell her coming pregnancy and the sex of the child. She wrote that she now uses this ability to help relatives.[33]

Through dream-reality work, you will be able to understand the meaning of your own dream language. This will give you a great advantage over people who do not observe their dreams. On one hand you will be guided through your life, especially through critical times, and on another hand the knowledge conveyed in dreams will contribute to alleviating the effects of bad news or difficulties you may have to face. Dreams will give you the opportunity to avoid avoidable problems. If a problem is unavoidable, dreams will prepare you to efficiently confront it. You will be better able to deal with the shock of bad news. When I make important life decisions, most often, the theme of the "road" appears in my dreams.

These dreams guide me. Sometimes I learn through them that I am on the wrong path, or they show me the correct path. The *greater consciousness* advice conveyed by dreams is of great value, because it is based upon much more information than is available to the conscious mind. Moreover, these dreams (and the *greater consciousness*) show more wisdom than the conscious mind, which lacks neutrality. The conscious mind manifests strong desires for the limited immediate aims it is able to foresee using reason. The *greater consciousness* is better informed than the *conscious mind*. It makes better decisions because it has access to information on the present, past and future. However you must learn to distinguish premonitory dreams from desire achievement dreams and recurring catastrophic nightmares. In some ways, Freud was right when he said that dreams are for desire achievement. This kind of dream occurs when we greatly desire something. In consequence if it is your case, do not take your dreams of desire achievement for "true" premonitory dreams. If you do so, you will be very disappointed. These dreams appear to be formed mainly by the conscious mind.

I notice that when I strongly want something and that I am too attached to it, my dreams generally cannot help me, because they are too influenced by my *conscious mind*. However my relatives are of great help, and often they dream the solution for me, particularly if they are not aware of my problems. In this case, their neutrality allows them to pick up the information in my *greater consciousness* better than me. My strong desire blocks this information from entering my conscious mind. In fact the more we are detached and neutral about our life concerns the more clearly we see the past, present and future through dreams and in reality. But being neutral is not always easy. Help from others is valuable. We also mentioned the necessity of distinguishing premonitory dreams from recurrent catastrophic nightmares. Some nightmares seem to announce many kind of catastrophic events like wars, earthquakes etc... It is important to keep in mind that most of the time these dreams do not announce the future. Very often they are the consequences of psychological trauma. This trauma can be ancient, and research in psychology has shown (through group-analysis) that in some families, this trauma can pass from generation to generation.[34] These nightmares have generally the same emotional theme though the scenes are ever changing. Some dreamers can feel a very strong fear, some other an indescribable anxiety and so on. These nightmares are unpleasant, but they give you a unique opportunity to reach information on the events which caused a trauma in yourself or in your family. Nightmares can be used as "hyperlinks" to reach key information on consciously forgotten traumas. If you can distinguish these nightmares from other types of nightmares, this will help you overcome them. Dream-reality work can help you greatly with this. Through this work you will be able to perceive which real events reactivate your traumatic memory. You may notice that stress alone can reactivate traumatic memories and give rise to horrible nightmares which in turn increase your stress. You may also observe that isolation can also reactivate them. Through these observations you will be able to go to the source of the traumatic memory usually unreachable to your conscious mind.[35] If you know the root of the problem, you can more easily rid yourself of these nightmares. Doctor Bach's flower remedies or other homeopathic remedies can help you. They heal "emotions" without side effects.[36] Healing emotions is the key to healing nightmares, regardless of their imagery. With practice you can verify which remedies are effective for your particular goals. For example, when I want to purify myself, I use the flower remedy named "Crab Apple". I can see through my dreams that it works because the theme of many of my dreams is "cleaning". In my dreams, I deep clean my house, the streets of Paris, and one day I guess I will even clean the Eiffel tower! Finally, regarding premonitory dreams, I would like to talk about fate.

Do not be fatalistic and resigned

Here I am going to make the same comparison as the one I used to explain premonitory dreams. We have seen that in the waking state we spend a lot of time scheduling the future, and that everybody finds it to be perfectly normal that we can in some way foretell future events. We have also seen that the main difference between the conscious mind and the greater consciousness in foretelling the future is that the greater consciousness benefits from much more information than the conscious mind. Therefore, the greater consciousness can plan a near or remote future with more accuracy. In waking life, we often schedule future events or meetings that are ultimately cancelled. For example, on Monday you take an appointment with a friend for the following Saturday and you cancel this appointment on Friday. Until Friday you knew your future regarding Saturday and yet this (waking life) prediction did not come true because you changed your mind. The same phenomenon occurs with respect to the predictions of your greater consciousness. The greater consciousness can modify its schedule, and you can ask it to "change its mind".

Whatever your dreams announce, do not be fatalistic and resigned. If it is true that dreams shape reality, reality also shapes dreams. Therefore, when something unpleasant is forming in the dream state, you can usually still take appropriate steps in the waking state to avoid the manifestation of these unpleasant things or to limit their negative consequences.[37] Most often, we are free to change our reality. This can be compared to the concept of karma in Buddhism: we can change negative Karma with appropriate measures if it is not too late. Here is a more practical example: it is possible to heal a physical problem as it begins, before it transforms itself in an incurable illness. And this leads us to the subject of dreams and health.

3. A different approach to medicine

Even today, Chinese medicine still takes into consideration the dreams of the patient in diagnosing a medical problem. Modern western medicine is far from sharing this attitude though dream interpretation with a medical aim was common in the west during antiquity.[38] In the Greco-Roman world, the sick used to go to the temples of Aesclepios, God of medicine, to find a solution to their health problems through dreams. Priests received them and had them perform purification rites. When the priest judged a person ready, he allowed the person to sleep in the temple. There, the sick person would then often receive a solution from the god Aesclepios in a dream. In the course of history, priests began to play the role of dream interpreter. Today, we do not need to believe in Aesclepios, nor go to temples, nor depend on a clergy to understand dream messages.[39] Through your dream-reality work, you will see that healing dreams are not miraculous. Multi-level health "scanning" (that is to say: physical health, energy health and mental health) is one of the major natural functions of the *greater consciousness*. Unfortunately, few people study their dreams and it would be unthinkable to teach this in medical schools. Through my dream-reality work I have learned a lot about health. But, above all, I have become conscious of the importance of the energy aspect of human life. As modern medicine has rediscovered through the concept of "psychosomatic" illnesses, body and mind are intimately connected. Psychological problems can manifest themselves in physical discomforts, and inversely a physical shock can give rise to a psychological trauma. Most of the time, illnesses result from a mix of physical and psychological causes. Due to the close connection between body and mind, it is possible through the dream-reality work to better understand how the body functions in connection with the mind. We can use dreams to diagnose the cause of existing health problems or to prevent the physical manifestation of illnesses that are announced in dreams. An illness is never mere coincidence, and does not form itself all of a sudden. Fortunately the body can endure our mistakes for some time before manifesting physical disorders. If not, we would die very easily from the abuse we impose on our bodies. Through your dream-reality journal you will see that physical disorders exist at first on a psychological or energy level within your *greater consciousness*, and then, if you do not take appropriate measures in due time, they manifest themselves in "real life". You will also see that one of the major functions of dreams is to convey information on the dreamer's health to the conscious mind, in order to aid in self-preservation. This is the dream counterpart of the powerful instinct of self-preservation. Illnesses are not fatalities which happen specifically to you or to your family, all of a sudden. You (or your family) have been preparing the illness for some time, even if sometimes it seems to occur all of a sudden. I am always surprised to see to what extent most people ignore their bodies just as they ignore their dreams and their inner lives. Instead of causing us suffering, dreams, body and inner life can be our best allies provided we observe them properly. However, people are so afraid of them and ignorant of how they function, that they often prefer not to confront them. Such an attitude is not good. It tends to create a continuous state of anxiety, a fear of solitude and of silence, and a great dependency on the presence of other people. By changing this attitude, people can regain peacefulness, avoid many miseries, and see for themselves how useful dreams are as allies. They should take advantage of dreams, instead of being afraid of them. Dreams show in advance physical, psychological and energy problems before they have consequences in the physical world.[40] I know from my experience what dreams of hair or teeth loss mean to me, and I take appropriate steps to avoid the real discomfort they are announcing. I also know, for example, that I must not worry if I dream that I am bald-headed, and that my legs are hairy when I have spent some time in the company of someone with these traits. If this occurs, I know I have simply picked up sensations from this individual! With the sensitivity I have developed through my dream-reality work, I may pick up information on health problems forming in people around me. In the beginning, I believed this information was related to my own health, but in time I have come to better know my own health context and to distinguish between information concerning me and information concerning others. Through the dream-reality work you can help other people by picking up from their *information sphere* the information they are not able to be conscious of by themselves. But you will see that it is not a pleasant task, as you will feel all their discomforts in the dreaming state. Nevertheless, when you are sufficiently advanced you can decide to use your dream ability to help the people less advanced than you or too anxious or fearful to see by themselves. Anxiety, stress, agitation, hatred and other negative emotions distort and blur the reception of dream messages by the conscious mind. As we have shown in the diagram (n°4) dreams are an intermediary between the *greater consciousness* and the *conscious mind*. In consequence they can be influenced by both consciousnesses. If you are flexible and open, if your mind is clear and peaceful, you will get more opportunities to get crystal clear dreams. One does not need to use the lucid dreaming techniques to realize how much the conscious mind remains active in the dream state. There, through dream-reality work, you can see that it can reject, judge and change, the information it finds unsuitable or unpleasant. Fortunately, in the dream state, the conscious mind is not as powerful as it is in "real life" and therefore dreams always remain a rich and valuable source of information, especially in the fields of health and energy preservation. I have seen through my dream-reality journal, that **the main concern of the *greater consciousness* is preservation of life force, that is to say energy**. Without life-force even a perfect body is not a living being. When energy is low, the body can function, and we can live an almost "normal" life but feelings of life emptiness will occur and can give rise to depression and mental illnesses. On the other hand, when energy is high this gives rise to physical and spiritual well being and happiness. There are many ways to pick up energy and there is an abundance of energy in the atmosphere, it is everywhere around us, the only thing we need is to be open to it. Dream-reality work is one way to be more open to life-energy. There are many other ways too: for example, doing a job you like is a powerful way to open yourself to life-force. You have certainly already experienced difficulty waking up when unpleasant tasks are awaiting you. On such days you feel tired, and even sometimes depressed. The opposite happens when you have interesting things to do or interesting people to meet. On the level of energy, doing a job you like and which suits you will give you an energy recharge while working. On the other hand, if you do a job you do not like you will feel drained of energy. By forcing yourself to do things you do not like you block the energy flow inside the body and experience all the bad consequences we have already mentioned. People who have found their calling and have the courage to live it in spite of the many obstacles, feel content and blissful in a way that no physical wealth can bring. Unfortunately, education, family context, material problems and sometimes collective problems like war, prevent many people from following their deep calling.

Everyone has a calling and dreams are a means of helping discover it. Doing so can give a sense to your life again. It is never too late to do what we love, and on an energy level doing so is always beneficial. Doing things we like allows energy to circulate and helps us overcome psychological problems which have occurred due to conflicts in our lives between our deepest needs and the actual lives we were living. When you live the real life you deeply need, you have a blissful feeling, and a sensation of peacefulness, and quietness, even when confronted by new problems. What's more, if you follow your calling, this will contribute to maintaining good health and to increasing energy. This will bring about the reactivation of some unused mental abilities. A lack of energy can manifest itself in physical discomfort but also in the increasingly common modern inner discomfort of depression. People confronted with depression for one reason or another, do not have enough life energy. In other words, we can say they are not alive enough. On the contrary, when a person is full of inner energy his/her life appears joyful and pleasant, even if the physical conditions of life are not ideal. This kind of inner well-being renders people very attractive, though one cannot explain why, on a material level. Such well-being is never the result of material wealth, but always comes from the ability to open oneself to the flow of life-energy. In our overly materialistic modern world, which does not pay attention to life force, it is not surprising that energy disorders have become a major social problem. In France, for example, there is a high suicide rate and many depressive people have become dependent on tranquillizers and antidepressants in order to live a "normal life". They are often deprived of dreams due to the side effects of the drugs they use.[41] The United States is another country where this problem occurs. Through the dream-reality work, one can learn to better manage his/her energy. Dreams can help you improve your life, and will

cause you to radiate happiness and energy, which will make you more attractive independently of your physical appearance. Dream-reality work will help you understand that some places or some activities help you recharge energy, while other places or activities decrease your energy. It is up to you to make your own observations, keeping in mind that everyone is unique and that a place can be good for one person and very bad for someone else. We have different needs. The same phenomenon occurs with the people we meet. Here, even without observing dreams, we know that some persons are exhausting and we avoid them whenever we can. Sometimes we feel guilty doing so because these individuals pretend to love us or seem friendly and sociable. A person with a very low energy level cannot do you good, this is why depressed people are not attractive people and that despite religious precepts many people follow their instincts and avoid them. I believe that humanity will better manage the problem of low energy in the future. We will develop the right conditions for maintaining high levels of life-energy and the technology to better help people. In the meanwhile, if you have a high energy level, you can decide to help depressed people, alone or with a group. If you choose to do this you will lose energy in his/her favor just from mixing your energy fields. Low energy levels may have numerous causes. These causes vary in importance and can be combined, like:
- places that drain your energy
- colors that depress you,
- personal psychological problems,
- unhealthy diet
- unhealthy life style
- people acting as energy parasites
- ignorance of recharge mechanisms
- group effect
- boring life

When a person's life energy level is low, this person becomes repulsive to people with good preservation instincts, whatever his/her age, physical appearance, or social status. This is not flattering for the individuals with low life-energy, but it is a reality. You will see through your dream-reality journal the existence, on the level of energy, of some "dead places" and of some "dead souls" as Gogol entitled one of his novels. In addition, modern food is increasingly "dead" on an energy level. We are constantly confronted with energy losses, and with energy disturbances as modern cities were built without knowledge of the intangible. Our body is very sensitive to the effects of energy differences yet few people are conscious of their occurrence. Modern science is gradually recognizing them: for example, it is increasingly accepted that the presence of high tension electric lines in the vicinity of houses can cause health problems like cancers to the inhabitants of these houses. We will have to wait some time before science becomes advanced enough to better account for the energy side of health. In the meantime, we can benefit from dreams which never ignore energy problems. Energy preservation is such a great concern for the *greater consciousness* that dreams can often signal energy problems in a terrifying and exaggerated manner. For example, a poorly operating electric device beside your bed can provoke a nightmare in which you are surrounded and attacked by bats. In the nightmare state, you can feel how the bats, which symbolize the energy disturbance are hurting you, but when you wake up terrified you become once again insensitive to the energy disturbance caused by the poorly operating electric device beside your bed. Therefore, you may continue to have the same kind of nightmares until you repair the electric device. Regarding nightmares, one should be practical and try to eliminate at first all the material causes that can provoke them, like bad position of bed, electric devices, proximity to high tension electric lines, etc... After having checked all the physical and material causes (nightmares can also be due to bad digestion or to health problems in formation), if the nightmares continue and are not due to a personal psychological conflict you should sleep alone for a while to check if the nightmares continue. Indeed in many cases nightmares are caused by the presence of other people in the place where we usually sleep. Though nightmares are very unpleasant they are the best way for our *greater consciousness* to be heard and to help us preserve our life. The *greater consciousness* is our best ally. It is probably what so many spiritual traditions represent as the guardian angel. Like a guardian angel, your *greater consciousness* takes care of your life, guides you and warns you of dangers, moreover you can ask it all the information you want. I would like now to speak of an efficient way, which I have experienced, of getting the information you need from your *greater consciousness*.

Chapter 4: How you can use the dream-reality connections

1. A powerful tool for accessing information

After doing dream-reality work for some time, you will be able to understand almost all your dream vocabulary. You will possess a remarkably efficient means to get the information and the advice you want from your *greater consciousness*.

Indeed, you will be able to speak with your greater consciousness in its proper language and will communicate better with it. We have seen that the dream is the mediator between the greater consciousness and the conscious mind. We all receive information from the greater consciousness through dreams, as schematized below (diagram n° 9):

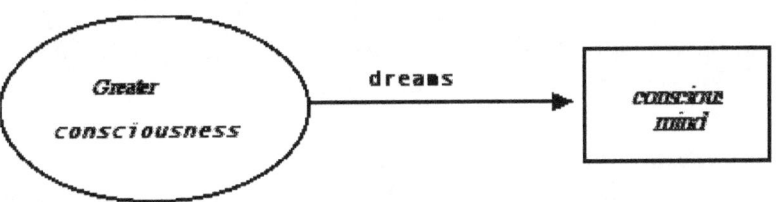

Because the dream is the mediator between the *greater consciousness* and the conscious mind, it is also possible to use the dream in reverse, that is to say from the conscious mind to the *greater consciousness*, as schematized below (diagram n° 10):

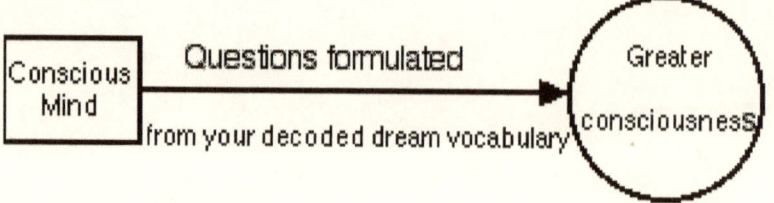

In fact, this occurs naturally, because the conscious mind also sends information to the *greater consciousness*. But by using your own dream vocabulary you will improve communication between your conscious mind and your *greater consciousness*. Before falling asleep, ask yourself questions formulated from your decoded dream vocabulary. When you use the dream language to ask your *greater consciousness* a question, this significantly increases your chances of getting an accurate dream answer, unlike asking the same question in conscious mind language.

2. *Using the dream-reality connection to improve your life*

Let us take the example of a common modern concern: employment. If you have deciphered through dream-reality work that the dream symbol "hat" stands for your job, you will be able to use this same symbol in the reverse direction, from the conscious mind to the *greater consciousness*. Thus the symbol "hat" will form part of the question you ask yourself before falling asleep, like: "Am I going to change hats?" I have noticed that an efficient way to get answers is to form images in your mind, while asking yourself the question using your decoded dream symbols. You will learn that asking questions with your heart, that is, to load them with emotion (full of life-energy) is very efficient.

3. Accelerating the path of scientific innovation

If I were doing scientific research, I would use my ability to dream to make discoveries instead of spending most of my time simply researching. It has always amused me that France only has a National Research Center and not a National Discoveries Center. The National Research center employs people to spend considerable time on unsuccessful research. The researchers are much too serious and much too busy to observe their dreams. Unfortunately, in the field of science, few people have developed their intuition and very few pay attention to their dreams. However in order to create, one must dare to dream. Fortunately, some famous scientific discoverers have recognized the main role played by dreams and intuition in the discovery process[42]. According to them, rationality alone does not give rise to scientific discoveries. On the contrary, dreams and intuition have given rise to the most important discoveries in the history of humanity. According to successful researchers, the mental process of scientific creativity takes place in two steps: first, an idea or a piece of intuitive information or a dream pops up, in a second step, thanks to logic and experimentation this idea, intuition or dream is tested in the reality and sometimes this gives rise to accepted scientific discoveries.

Though uncommon, innovative dreams have existed for ever. Few modern researchers dare to speak of them because of taboos about the brain's abilities (like intuition or dreams) imposed by the scientific establishment. The attitude of the larger public and of scientists themselves about innovative dreaming is quite irrational. Whenever the existence of an innovative dream is admitted it is attributed, as in "primitive" humanity, to a kind of divine intervention which we today call "luck" or "chance". Nobody tries to understand the process of innovative dreaming: why did a determined researcher have an innovative dream or an innovative idea? And yet, upon closer observation, an innovative idea, dreamed or not, never comes at random, it necessarily results from a set of circumstances favorable to its occurrence. Inversely, the low rate of discoveries is a result of a set of circumstances obstructing scientific discovery. If researchers had developed their dream skills, they would be able to understand the existing obstructions to their creativity. They would learn to place themselves into the situations that are more conducive to scientific discovery. The method consisting in asking the *greater consciousness* questions using the decoded dream vocabulary would be of particular use in scientific research. Scientists using this method would have an efficient means to access information stored in the *greater consciousness*. And much more information is available to the *greater consciousness* than to the conscious mind, which can only proceed through random research. Sadly so-called scientific rationality does not allow scientists to escape the too narrow limits of the conscious mind. Though more and more scientists are opening themselves to brighter horizons,[43] modern science denies the existence of any human abilities that it cannot explain or measure from a materialistic angle. This remains true despite abundant proofs that these abilities exist. They have been developed by individuals at every stage of human history. The study of dreams and the technique of hypnosis demonstrate that these abilities are dormant in humans but can be reawakened. But prior to being able to do that you will need to practice for a while and acquire "dream hygiene". You will learn not to obstruct your dreaming process.

4. Avoiding obstructions to the good functioning of your dream process

When you overload your brain with outer information (too much reading, movie watching, television, radio, or contacts), you can spend your nights "digesting" information consciously acquired during your waking life. In doing so, you diminish your chances of receiving dreams prompted by the *greater consciousness*. When this occurs the "dream-space" is busy digesting information from the conscious mind, and dreams are subjected to most of the limitations of the conscious mind. This is what happens to the vast majority of modern humanity. A healthy mental life implies time for solitude and silence in order to "digest" the information received by your conscious mind and to free your inner dream-space in order to receive messages from your *greater consciousness*. Another very practical obstacle to the occurrence of creative and "answering" dreams is great fatigue and not enough sleep. If you sleep only the time necessary to physically recharge, the quality and your memory of dreams will be diminished. You will notice that you get your best creative and "answering" dreams in the morning, especially when you fall asleep again. Deep fatigue is a great obstacle to remembering dreams. On another level, overeating or eating greasy foods can cause you to spend your night having very physical dreams and often digestive nightmares. Try it yourself, compare the quality of your dreams in different circumstances: for example, when you are in top physical and mental condition, when you are extremely tired, or when you feel depressed. Give as much comfort as you can to your physical body, so that your body does not require it in your dreams and so that you get the highest quality sleep possible. Working on the connection between your dreams and your reality is very rewarding. When you have deciphered your unique dream language, you will possess a powerful key to accessing an immense data bank the existence of which you had probably ignored. Though we are proud to have entered the information and communication age, humanity as a whole uses only a very small portion of the existing information. This is because brains are not developed enough to access all this information. Dream-reality work points out what the real abilities of the brain are. These abilities will be developed and used in the waking state, by the humanity of the future.

Chapter 5: A new philosophy of mind

1. *What makes our brain work?*

It was generally believed that we use only around 10 % of the brain's capability.[44] But modern neuroscientists now say that this idea is a myth and that it is very difficult to assert how much of the brain is actually activated. Some neuroscientists have ridiculed those who believe that the brain has "paranormal" faculties. Why should we believe these specialists? Their knowledge comes mainly from observing animals in laboratories. They do not pay attention to their dreams or their inner lives. In my opinion, they are at an impasse for they study the brain in an isolated manner. Sound study of the dreaming process has shown how each brain, as part of the invisible human network, is constantly interacting with other brains in the network, and can be deeply affected by its intangible environment. Moreover, focusing mainly on the number of neurons that are activated does not seem to entirely explain intelligence. For example we read in scientific studies that the poor memory of the elderly is probably linked to the significant loss of neurons which occurs after the age of 30. This is a quantitative materialistic approach to the brain. On the contrary, with good sense you can see for yourself that the functioning of your brain is strongly linked to your energy level. For example, when you have not slept enough, your memory is less accurate. You can also easily see that your faculties can vary greatly depending on the people you interact with, for example the presence of some people can block your imagination or instead boost it. On another level, if it is true that everyone from the age of 30 losses so many neurons, why do we find such a high disparity in mental condition between elderly people or even between young people deemed to have equivalent numbers of neurons? The quantity of activated neurons does not explain the levels of intelligence, moreover if neurons were so important, the body would not rid itself of them. My intuition is that with regard to intelligence, though neurons are necessary, quality and level of life-energy are more important than the quantity of neurons.

2. *Which capacities of the conscious mind energize us the most?*

In order to keep our brains in good condition, neurologists advise us to keep our brains active by: reading, writing, calculating and doing physical exercise to oxygenate the brain. Neurologists do not distance themselves enough from our civilization. Not every civilization needed writing and reading. For example, Ancient Egypt was mostly a civilization of symbols where writing played an insignificant role. With our modern intelligence, we are still unable to understand the meaning of most of their symbols. They simply used their intelligence differently. When neurologists make the *third choice* and consider life both in its tangible and intangible aspect, they will be able to make considerable progress understanding the real functioning of the brain. They will become able to propose effective remedies without the side effects of modern brain medication. For now, we do not need neurology to see that the modern world is unbalanced because memory, and rationality are highly valued, to the detriment of imagination and intuition. You can easily see for yourself that "pure rationality" is not connected to life-energy, rather, emotions, love and communication are powerful captors of life-force. In fact our whole civilization is imbalanced. This is particularly true in developed countries and particularly in France. In the country of Descartes, we greatly value engineers, formed in schools where intuition is useless. By choosing memory and rationality to the detriment of imagination, intuition and sensitivity, humanity cannot reach the level of life-energy necessary to give rise to unusual brain faculties. It is as if we were using only one leg. We cannot walk and we cannot run. Because we value skills acquired from only one of the hemispheres of the brain, we do not know what "to walk" and even less what "to run" mean to the brain. With the development of information technology, humanity can rely upon computers for memory and rationality and thus can free its energy for developing other abilities. Students all over the world have understood this, and they use modern technology to cheat.[45] Instead of fighting against this trend with the same technology, society as a whole should take some distance and understand the message: "it's time to rethink the philosophy of 'schools' and of life!" Memory and rationality can be the job of the computers, we no longer need to value them so much. Instead we should improve our teaching of how to awaken the skills linked to imagination, intuition and personal growth. The dream-reality work can contribute to awaken these skills. This work is indeed a particularly simple means of personal development. It is efficient and safe. It allows us to live a normal life while achieving personal growth. Everyone can use this method in his/her own way, with his/her own nuances. Everybody can profit from it: rich or poor, rational or intuitive, religious or not. Among the multiple benefits you can draw from the dream-reality work:

- you can better understand your personal psychological problems and therefore have more opportunities to solve them and to remove energy blocks;
- you can learn how to better manage your energy, as dream-reality work shows how energy is lost and how it is gained;

- you can better understand the people around you as you will get more information on them than you would through the conscious mind alone;
- you will be able to diagnose, prevent or find a remedy to your health problems; or to help your doctor in this way;
- you will be better able to find your way in life, as the dream-reality work provides you with more information on the past, present and valuable information on your future immediate or remote; even when this future cannot be logically expected from your present life;
- you will be able to regain awareness of forgotten events in your life or in your family's life, which will help you better understand your present life;
- you will develop yourself on an energy level and therefore on a spiritual level;
- you will develop the unexploited intelligence that allows telepathy, intuition, clairvoyance, etc..
- you will be able to improve communication with people, and also with animals in both the dream and waking states.

There is no end to the list of advantages that dream-reality work offers because human intelligence, unlike the material brain, is unlimited. You can use this method to achieve whatever specific personal aim. If, for example, I were an archaeologist, instead of randomly digging, I would begin my work with a good nap. Due to my training in dream-reality work, my dreams during this nap would certainly give me clear information or strong intuition on where and how to dig.[46] Once I had found archeological remains, I would hold them in my hands for some time in order for my body to pick up "fresh" information on them, before they to museums. Once in the museums, these remains would be also impregnated with the information emanating from visitors and from the museum.

3. The collective awakening of a different kind of intelligence

Some capabilities are so dormant in the majority of the human beings that many people deny their reality. When some are able to experience them directly, they generally attribute this to divine intervention, miracles or supernatural powers. However these abilities are simply unexploited natural abilities. Abilities like telepathy and clairvoyance will be widely developed within the humanity of the future. That is to say, humanity as a whole will develop them and they will be regarded as natural phenomena. At the same time this future humanity will be also able to "measure" and increase the level of "life-energy" or "psychic-energy" of individuals and groups. We will be able to deal more effectively with depressed people by helping them understand why they have an energy deficit and helping them recharge their energy. Nowadays, everyone finds it normal that telephones allow communication at a distance. An invention such as cell phones would have been regarded as sorcery in the Middle Age and banned. The inventors and the courageous users would have been burned at the stake with all their odds and ends! Telephones and all the means of communication we have invented are material manifestations or prosthesis of the possibilities of the brain. Our body is much better at communicating than an assemblage of plastic and electronics which cannot receive life-energy. Think about that and observe your dreams, you will see that telepathy is a very common thing, but at the same time you will notice that telepathy is not what one generally believes it is. Telepathy allows us to receive and to emit emotions, images and energy charges.[47] The dream-reality work I have done caused an increase in my telepathic abilities. I still have progress to make, though I am now able to perceive at a distance thoughts that people are emitting about me, even if these persons are geographically very far from me. I have observed that my "new" mental abilities in the waking state vary with my energy level and my degree of peacefulness. I have also observed that some people emit - often without being aware of it- such strong thoughts that I have the impression I could almost touch them. It is easy for most of us to send powerful thoughts into the atmosphere, but it is very hard to find people able to perceive thoughts in the waking state. Therefore, it is not easy to find partners for telepathy training, in the waking state! First of all most people would think you are crazy and those open enough to try, would be able to emit but probably not to receive messages.[48] Many animals are much better at telepathy than humans. This means of communication probably existed before the invention of language.[49] Some cats, for example, by other means than meowing are very clever at perceiving thoughts and emitting them.[50] Lydia Hiby, who specializes in communicating with animals, believes that telepathy is a means of communication we all experienced before learning to speak.[51] And Helen Wambach,[52] a psychoanalyst who specialized in hypnosis, asserted that the most important thing she learned in her career was that: "words are a screen of smoke..." "real communication, (she stressed), occurs telepathically, under the level of words".[53] Telepathic communication consists in being able to emit and receive feelings, emotions, images, and symbols energetically charged. In order to emit thoughts in a satisfying way, you must have enough energy and/or a strong desire to communicate. In order to receive information in the telepathic way, you must be open, notably have an open heart, that is to say emotional sensitivity. Of course, if you believe that telepathy exists, this is much better. A person with a mind and a sensitivity closed to telepathy is like a person who does not hear the ring or the vibration of his/her cell phone and therefore does not answer, while his/her *greater consciousness*, like an answering machine, records the messages. Some of these messages will pass to the conscious mind, more or less distorted, through dreams. Lydia Hiby writes that when she communicates with animals, she receives the information by her higher self.[54] At the beginning of my research, I also believed that telepathy was a paranormal faculty. I now believe, that the human senses and the corresponding abilities of the brain, are far more extended than what we can imagine from a materialistic approach to life. There is still much to learn about the unexploited human intelligence, but now let us come to the conclusion of this study.

Conclusion

In this book, instead of excluding one dimension of life to the benefit of the other, I have chosen to give equal importance to the tangible and the intangible sides of life. I have called this the *third choice*. This angle has allowed to point the permanent existing interactions between these two aspects of life. Archaeological remains and traces in Roman law show that some ancient civilizations already made this choice. Ancient Roman legal procedure still bears testimony to this fact, for the Romans took into account the diverse effects of the laws of action on the tangible and the intangible. The application of this ancient wisdom to the observation of the dreaming process has opened new horizons, and has widened the usual narrow scope in which dreams have always been studied. This has allowed us to achieve the following results:

1°: Understanding that the vast majority of dreams, like the vast majority of life processes in general, result from a process of exchange between the dreamer and his/her tangible and intangible environment. I have stressed throughout the book the role played by the human body as a whole, in the course of these exchanges, and explained how through a simultaneous observation of dreams and reality one can decipher one's own unique dream language, with more accuracy than with all the existing methods. Indeed, after a long enough period of time it becomes possible to decipher with accuracy most of your dreams, because the same dream symbols appear in connection with the same contexts in the waking state.

2°: I have observed that the latent capacities of the brain, usually regarded as "paranormal" or simply denied, are in fact very active in the dream state. As a result of the dream-reality work, these capacities can also be reawakened and used in the waking state, in a manner that is simple, safe, and accessible to all. One does not need a guru, expensive classes, and it is not dangerous as everyone follows his/her own path.

3°: I have observed that a relation exists between the development of these capacities of the conscious mind and the energy level of persons. This last observation is also applicable to humanity as a whole. The dream-reality work allows us to increase our energy potential for many reasons. It allows us, notably, to define and remove psychological blocks; to develop an awareness of energy problems and to learn how to solve them; and to reach a better understanding of the mechanism of energy recharge.

4°: I have noticed that memory extends much further than we can imagine, and that we have a kind of consciousness that is much more developed and powerful than that associated with the waking state, or conscious mind. Through the dream process, this bigger consciousness appears to program our brains for our daily life performances, and such programming is operative whether or not we remember our dreams. Unfortunately, many people do not follow this personal guidance, and in failing to do so they hinder the correct flow of their life-energy. The dream-reality work allows us to better understand our purpose in life. It leads to peacefulness and confidence, insofar as by paying attention to dreams, we obtain an insight into our next and sometimes remote future.

5° The dream-reality work has enabled us to see how

much better feelings, colors, images, emotions, and dreams convey our life force than all the rational activities of the mind. This allows us to understand why myths and symbols are so important for all the people we are accustomed to consider "primitive", as they have been more interested than we in the wealth of life-energy. Let us wager that, when humanity wakes up, the primitive people of the future will be our modern rational elites who have been unable to free themselves from the myth of pure reason.

Frequently asked questions

1: Why don't I dream?

It has now been scientifically proved that everyone dreams except people with damaged brains. Dreaming is necessary to good physical and mental health. If you believe you do not dream, do not worry. It is very easy to reactivate the memory of dreams.[55] At the beginning of your dream-reality work, if you cannot remember the scenery and the content of your dreams, just write down your feelings when you wake up. Observe your mood and take notes about it. Are you happy, sad, peaceful? Also take note of your physical state: are you in good physical condition, or do you feel tired? As soon as you wake up, note the thoughts wandering in your mind. Of course, do not immediately think about daily life concerns. Obviously, if Vanessa is your name and your radio-clock wakes you up with "good morning Simone", your mind will immediately focus on understanding why the sudden change of identity! In the same way, if instead of thinking about your dreams, you immediately think about daily life concerns, your chances of remembering your dreams will decrease. The more interested you are in your dreams, the easier they are to remember. Memory of your dreams rapidly increases when you pay attention to dreams. A good "side effect" of dreams observation consists in the simultaneous improvement of memory during the waking state. The reverse is true too, by improving your memory during the waking state you can improve the memory of your dreams. If you are unable to remember your dreams through one of the means mentioned above, you can think about asking someone who dreams and remembers well his/her dreams, to help you. The presence of this person will stimulate your own system. By spending some time with this person you will stimulate your own "dream process". Human exchanges are not limited to material things, words and gestures, they are much more extended than what we can imagine. On a practical ground, if you are very tired and sleep only enough for physical recovery, you will decrease the possibility of remembering your dreams and you will decrease the quality of your dreams. Another technique you can use is to tell yourself before you fall asleep: "I want to dream and I want to remember my dreams". This is very simple but effective. You can also change room or skip dinner. Here are some other means which I have not tried that have been proposed in dream literature:

In a book on the yoga of dreams: it is advised to allow more air and/or light to enter the place where you sleep; or to visualize a red sphere at the level of your throat, or a white bead on your forehead.[56]

In a book on lucid dreaming: it advises to add vitamin B6 to your diet, and use nutmeg to spice your food. It also advises the use of a pillow stuffed with dry mugwort (Artemisia vulgaris) or the use of Clary Sage oil (Salvia sclarea) which is hypnotic and should not be used in conjunction with alcohol or in conjunction with a pillow stuffed with dry mugwort. But this pillow should not be used by pregnant women as mugwort contains "a substance that can induce miscarriage".[57]

In a book written by a psychologist and dream therapist[58]: we can read that motivation is important and that heavy greasy foods, tobacco, alcohol and sleeping pills should be avoided as much as possible. The book also points out the bad effect on dream recall of being awakened by an alarm clock. This book proposes "the glass of water" method to help remember your dreams. You just put a glass of water beside your bed. Before going to sleep, you take a little sip of the water and while doing so suggest to yourself that upon awakening you will remember your dreams by drinking the rest of the water. It is stated that floral Elixirs (like: blackberry, forget-me-not, orange tree, apple tree), can help the dream process and that the Chaparral elixir from Deva's laboratories[59] is deemed to let repressed emotions reemerge. Dr. Bach's floral remedies are also mentioned. I have already spoken about floral remedies, it is very interesting to use them in dream-reality work. However, they are not at all compulsory because dreaming is a natural capability.

<u>In books from American dream-therapists</u>: It is suggested to stay still with your eyes closed upon awakening, and try to remember your dreams. Then it is advised to change your position in bed. This is deemed to facilitate dream recall. This advice is given by Patricia GARFIELD in her book *Creative Dreaming*.[60]

2: Why do I have nightmares?
Having nightmares is a very common though unpleasant experience which sometimes has bad effects on health. Instead of being afraid of dreams because of the possible occurrence of nightmares, we should try to understand why nightmares occur in order to be able to suppress the cause that provokes them. Nightmares result from many different causes linked to the physical and human environment, as well as bodily discomforts, or psychological conflict. In the field of nightmares, dream-reality work is very useful as it is the only way to understand the occurrence of some nightmares still unexplained by existing dream theories. We are going to list some of the causes of nightmares:

Physical causes linked to the dreamer's body and health: bad digestion, bad sleep posture, physical or breathing discomforts during the sleep, pain, illness, or a high amount of stress before going to sleep are common causes of nightmares.

Physical causes linked to the environment: malfunctioning electrical outlets, high tension electric cable near your house, too warm or too cold room, room with bad ventilation, the proximity of electric appliances, a badly located bed, the proximity of people incompatible with you can cause you nightmares. When you do not sleep alone, you can have the nightmares of your partner, or you can also have your own nightmares showing you in an exaggerated way that the energy exchange between you and the other person is not good for you.

Psychological reasons: nightmares linked to psychological problems are a very interesting subject of study through the dream-reality work. The simultaneous observation of dreams and reality will give you powerful help in going to the root of your problem, even if you have not the slightest conscious memory of traumatic psychological events. Though they are unpleasant, nightmares are the strongest "tool" the *greater consciousness* uses to show a big energy problem. This problem can be linked to psychological blocks due most of the time to forgotten childhood events and repressed emotions. So, do not be afraid of your nightmares, do not try to suppress them at once but better try to understand the information they convey. This can help you actually get rid of them and consequently increase your energy and well being. There is still a lot to discover about nightmares and especially about transgenerational nightmares which have been recently pointed out by modern psychologists. According to their observations there exists a transgenerational psychological heritage. This means that some nightmares can result from unresolved family problems which pass from generation to generation. Some of these problems can be linked to violence, family secrets, repressed emotions and family injustice. Through practical experience, Anne Ancelin Schützenberger, psychotherapist and group-analyst has been able to write about the existence of a kind of psychological heredity that Freud, she quotes, had called the "archaic heredity":[61]

In an interesting book,[62] Anne Ancelin Schützenberger, gives many examples, drawn from her practice of the existence of transgeneration psychological links. Many examples are given of nightmares had by the descendants of people who had been victims of traumatic events (related to war, accidents, rapes etc...) known or unknown to the descendants.[63] She observes that for now we cannot explain why some consciously unknown problems and traumas can bother several generations of a given family. The solution she proposes to overcome this kind of nightmare, is psychotherapy consisting in researching the family history and recovering consciousness of the events. A solution, such as forgiveness might be found to stop continued transmission to the next generation.

"Real" nightmares: what I call real nightmares are provoked by frightening or shocking information received and transmitted by the *greater consciousness*. For example if during a trip you sleep in a room where a murder took place, you may have a nightmare about this event. You may also have a nightmare due to the fact that you tune into some real frightening event taking place around you or happening to someone you know. You will find through dream-reality work that some locations are more favorable to the occurrence of nightmares because they are charged with the vibrations of events which have taken place in them. These events may have even occurred in a remote past. You will see that your *greater consciousness* is sensitive to these vibrations. Such places should be deep cleaned and purified, in order to change the atmosphere in the event that you cannot move to another place. Keep in mind that in case of long lasting incomprehensible nightmares, moving to another place may be the solution. A location can induce terrible nightmares in one person and have no effect on another because our sensitivities are different. The shamanistic approach to dreaming reckons the existence of psychic attacks and intrusions during sleep. This tradition advises us to take some preventive psychic protection measures to fight against psychic intrusion into our homes.[64] I can tell from experience that a high level of life-energy is the best shield against psychic intrusion.

"False" nightmares: What I call "false" nightmares are a certain number of nightmares which result from the narrowness of the conscious mind. During the dreaming state, our conscious mind, still active, can be frightened or shocked by symbolic dream content that it does not understand. The activity of a too narrow conscious mind during the dreaming process can give rise to emotions like fear, panic, and shame in front of dream imagery free from cultural prejudice. For example a person with strong sexual blocks in the waking state may be very shocked by some symbolic pornographic or incestuous dreams though the information conveyed by these dreams may have little to do with sex. Such a content will be lived as a nightmare by the dreamer though it is most often a very positive symbolic dream.

How to get rid of recurrent nightmares:
The ancient Greeks told their bad dreams to the sun whose light was deemed capable of destroying the effects of ill omens and the influences of bad spirits.[65] In some African countries people get rid of bad dreams by symbolically throwing them away.[66] In either case, this may work if you

believe it will. However, you will never understand why you had a nightmare, what the nightmare wanted to tell you, or how to put an end to recurrent nightmares. If you want to get rid of recurring nightmares, you must first, by process of elimination, determine what causes them. If the reason for your nightmares is physical, it will be easy to take the adequate physical measures to suppress the cause. For example if your recurring nightmare is provoked by a malfunctioning electrical outlet beside your bed, repairing the outlet in real life would be a better way to get rid of your nightmare than facing your dream enemies as some dream therapists advise. Facing dream enemies, overcoming them, then asking them for a present is a method suggested by Patricia GARFIELD who found it successful among the Senoï Malaysian tribe. Some other authors have experienced that facing their enemies in the dream state was very beneficial psychologically. Some authors advise on the other hand, to run away from the dream state and awaken in order to benefit from the security of real life.

As you can see, there is no unanimity on the topic. We still have a lot to discover about nightmares. At the same time, very few people think about using homeopathy which heals emotions without side effects. Nightmares and the emotions they convey can be used as a powerful diagnosis tool for choosing the right homeopathic remedies. Generally doctors in homeopathy do not pay attention to their clients' dreams. There may be emotions linked to physical disorder not expressed in the waking state, but in nightmares. By acknowledging the emotional content of nightmares one can select the appropriate homeopathic remedy. For example, when I was a very young child I was panicked when I had to cross a wooden bridge through which I could see the water. It was very painful... But, as a child, I was able to overcome this problem in reality and I was no longer afraid of crossing these kinds of bridges. However, as an adult, I noticed that some physical disorders which were very painful appeared at the same time as this nightmare, though I was not at all afraid to cross these bridges in the waking state. Using a homeopathic remedy appropriate to this kind of fear allowed me to solve the physical disorders linked to this painful emotion and to get rid of the recurring nightmare. You will observe through dream-reality work that, with time, recurring nightmares often induce physical disorders. Healing the painful emotional state and suppressing the nightmares in an intelligent manner will lead to healing the physical disorders too (obviously of not so obviously linked to the nightmares). There French expression "to have fear in the belly" is not a coincidence. If you have recurring nightmares full of intense fear, you may develop health problems in this part of the body. But the reverse is true too, if you have physical disorders in the digestive track, because of an unhealthy diet for example, you may have frightening nightmares connected to these physical problems. The physical and the psychological sides of the same problem interact with each other.

<u>Relaxation decreases the occurrence of nightmares</u>: You can see for yourself through the dream-reality work that intense stress in waking life can provoke terrible nightmares and that these terrible nightmares in turn can increase you waking life stress. If you have these kinds of nightmares it is important to learn how to relax and to avail yourself of the many techniques offered today to deal with stress, like: homeopathy, flower remedies, herbal remedies, relaxation techniques and aromatherapy, yoga.

3: How can I interpret my dreams?
At the beginning just write down your dreams and your reality without even trying to understand them. By doing

so you will develop a neutral and objective approach to the dream-reality connections. You will prepare yourself for a better understanding of your unique symbolic dream code and you will use both hemispheres of the brain. After a while, you will see that the same dream symbols appear in connection with the same real life situations. You can then deduce the precise meaning of your own dream symbols. Moreover, through comparing dreams to reality over a long period of time, you will notice that many dreams about your future were very clear and did not need to be interpreted. You will also notice that some dreams can only be explained in relation with your psychic environment. Nevertheless, if you are impatient to understand a new dream theme, you can try some dream-therapists' techniques. For example, the interview technique proposed by Gale Delaney is very interesting[67]. Robert Moss, on another hand, proposes to practice dream reentry to relive dreams.[68] But, do not trust dream dictionaries or other keys of dreams to help you understand your dreams. They will only mislead you and raise anxiousness. Every person has a unique dream language and personal work is necessary to decipher it and develop the capabilities of the brain. You will notice that throughout your life, there is relative stability in your dream language. You will decipher most of your dream language in the first years of your dream-reality work, later on you will learn new vocabulary, from time to time. The same occurs in the waking state when learning your mother tongue. New dream symbols linked to new real life situations will appear. Generally speaking, to understand new emerging dream vocabulary, never forget that the *greater consciousness* is rooted in nature and that many dream symbols can be understood with reference to natural processes. For example a growing plant appearing in a dream will stand for an increase in your real life (psychic, financial, or sentimental...). In nature water is strongly linked to life and life to energy, so dreams involving water can be understood in relation to life processes. On this level a dictionary of symbols is a very useful means to open your mind to the meaning of symbols. These dictionaries do not relate to dreams, they only list symbols and their meaning throughout history and in various civilizations.[69] Finally listen to your intuition and observe the emotions you experience in the dreaming state. Emotions are often the key to understanding the meaning of obscure dreams. They are also the key to accessing a greater memory.

4: What is a lucid dream?
Both in the dreaming and waking states, we can learn to live more consciously. We can decide to control the course of events, instead of passively living them. The lucid dreaming technique was employed long ago by Tibetans and by shamans. It has been recently rediscovered by the western world. Lucid dreaming has become popular in America thanks to the best sellers written by Carlos Castaneda and the scientific works of Stephen Laberge. Carlos Castaneda wrote that he had received teachings on lucid dreaming techniques from a South American sorcerer who he called "Don Juan". The aim of Castaneda's "art of dreaming" is spiritual. In his Californian laboratory, Stephen Laberge has studied the techniques of lucid dreaming in as systematic and scientific a way as possible. He has invented technical devices which can induce lucid dreams. In this case, lucid dreaming is studied for itself, out of curiosity and also for the pleasure that can be found in experiences that are impossible in real life, for example: flying. A common benefit of maintaining consciousness in the dreaming state is that lucid dreamers are able to consciously change the course of their dreams. For example, they can change a nightmare to a pleasant dream. The dominance of the *conscious mind* over the *greater consciousness* in lucid dreams is so strong that one might wonder if it is still a

dreaming state, and if such techniques are safe for the mind? On another ground, if we take the example of nightmares caused by information the body picks up in the environment, it may be a bad idea to change the course of the nightmare. Instead, it would be better, if possible, to take the necessary steps into the waking world. Lucid dreaming techniques can sometimes be useful. However, it would be safer to understand what the dream process is before trying to direct it and before submitting it to the limitations of the conscious mind. We must understand that dreaming is a process which occurs within an invisible web between all living beings and that a dreamer is never in a closed circuit. Dreams always result from and exchange with the environment immediate or remote. Nobody can live in full mental isolation. Dreams always have a direct link with the dreamer's real life and with his/her real environment, immediate or remote.[70] Lucid dreaming can happen without using specific techniques. Its frequency increases if you do dream-reality work. But most of the time, lucid dreaming results from the use of specific techniques and training. In the teaching of the Tibetan yoga of dreaming, dream lucidity is deemed to result from preliminary spiritual growth and particular spiritual practices. In the Tibetan tradition lucidity is sought and practiced to prepare oneself for the passage to death.[71] But modern western lucid dream seekers are mainly interested in events impossible in waking life, but experienced at will in the lucid dreaming state. What they seek through lucid dreaming is mainly travel, flight, discovery and most of all sexual freedom! Though lucid dreaming is very popular on the Internet, there are also some people warning about lucid dreaming. The author Gale Delaney (psychologist and dream-therapist) for example writes:

... I can say with no reservation that lucid dreaming does not equal spiritual or psychological superiority. I have worked with the dreams and the lives of gurus and others who have regular lucid dreams, and some of them have little psychological maturity, love, or generosity in their hearts. Others are indeed beautifully evolved people. Some people who focus great efforts on having as many lucid dreams as possible do so because they have an unhealthy need to control all their experiences and have little knowledge about who they really are. They avoid serious exploration of their inner feelings either through dream work or psychotherapy.[72]

If you are interested in lucid dreaming see the bibliography and the list of web sites on this subject. But, please, before trying these techniques first learn how your brain functions through the dream-reality work. I generally do not try to control my dreams with my conscious mind. Even when I am conscious in my dreams (which occurs more and more often) I let my *greater consciousness* operate as the results are richer and much more unexpected than what I can expect from the limited conscious mind. On another ground, I often use a kind of lucid dreaming to get information I need, without using induction techniques. But the dream process is so extensive that nobody can actually distinguish between a lucid dream, an out of the body experience, an astral travel, a projection of consciousness, etc... As you can see there is still a lot to discover, so do not limit yourself to theories on dreams. Try it yourself with an open mind, do not reject discoveries on the dreaming state without verifying them when you can do it. Keep your mind and your heart open to discovery of the life process of which dreams are parts.

5: When sleeping, can we only perceive the information from our immediate surroundings?
Yes the body does this all the time. Robert Moss also noticed this phenomenon he called "the psychic Internet".

In the dream state as well as in the waking state we are able to receive remote information. Insects, for example can perceive sexual partners that are very far away, thanks to hormones they emit in the air. The "law of attraction" plays a major role in reception of geographically remote information. Your immediate environment will influence the remote information you may receive. Specific kinds of remote information will be attracted to you according to the quality and the level of your energy.

Many authors and religious traditions have mentioned the fact that when we sleep we can go out of the body and live an out of the body life, meet people, travel etc... It is easy to verify this yourself through dream-reality work. You will notice that during this kind of dream, your physical body remains active, receiving and emitting information. Some modern researchers have explored techniques to go out of the body at will. They have called this Out of the Body Experiences or OBE. This is yet another vast and ancient question which reveals how unlimited the human mind is and how little we know about it.

BIBLIOGRAPHY

Modern books about dreams

Delaney Gale, *All About Dreams, Everything You Need to Know About Why We Have Them, What They Mean, and How To Put Them to Work for You,* New York, Harper Collins, Harper Sanfrancisco, 1988. Website: www.GDelaney.COM
Founder of the The Association for The Study of Dreams, www.outreach.org/gmcc/asd.
(Psychological approach)

GODWIN Malcom, *The Lucid Dreamer, A Waking Guide For the Traveller Between Worlds*, Shaftesbury, Labyrinth Publishing, 1994.(Lucid dreaming approach)

HOBSON J. Allen, *The Dreaming Brain*, Penguin, 1990 (Scientific approach)

KELSEY Morton, *Dreams: A Way to Listen to God*, New York/Mahwah, Paulist Press, 1989, (Religious approach)
Laberge Stephen and RHEINGOLD Howard, *Exploring the World of Lucid Dreaming*, New York, Ballantine Books, 1992, (Lucid dreaming approach)

Moss Robert , *Dreaming True, How to Dream Your Future and Change Your Life for the Bette*r, New York, Pocket Books, September 2000, www.mossdreams.com
(Shamanic approach)

NORBU NamKhai, *Dream Yoga and the Practice of Natural Light*, New York, Snow Lion Publications, 1992. (French translation Le *Yoga du Rêve*, Paris, J.L. Accarias, 1993, collection L'originel, translation by arrangement with Snow Lion Publications, Ithaca, New York 14851, Editor KATZ,Michel translation by GAUDEBERT Gisèle).(Yoga approach)

WOODS Ralph L. and GREENHOUSE Herbert B., Editors, *The New World of Dreams*, New York, Macmillan Publishing Co, inc., second printing 1974, (Scientific approach).

Ancient literature and "classical" literature on dreams

Aristotle, *La Vérité des songes, De la divination dans le sommeil*, (Parva naturalia 462 b - 464 b), translated and presented by Jackie Pigeaud, Paris, Rivages Poche, 1995

Artemidorus, *The Interpretation of Dreams: Oneirocritica*, Translated by R. J. White, Park Ridge, N.J., Noyes Press, 1975

E. R. Dodds, *Les Grecs et l'irrationnel*, Paris, Aubier, 1965. "Supernormal phenomena in Classical Antiquity", in *The Ancient Concept of Progress and other Essays on Greek Literature and Belief*, Clarendon Press, Oxford, 1973

Freud Sigmund, *The Interpretation of Dreams*, New York: Avon Books, 1965 (first publication in 1900) (psychology)

Jung Carl Gustav,*Memories, Dreams and Reflections*, London, Routledge and Kegan paul, 1963 (psychology)

Saint-Denis H., *Dreams and How to Guide Them*, London, Duckworth, 1982. (Lucid dreaming)

Organisations and websites about dreams

http://www.cgjungpage.org
http://www.dreamdoctor.com
http://www.Dreamtree.com
http://members.tripol.com/enchantco/dreamchat/id2.htm
chat@asdreams.org
dreamchatters@yahoogroups.com list
http://www.yahoogroups.com/group/dreamchatters for more info
http://www.dreamgate.com/electric-dreams
The Association for the Study of Dreams ADS
:http://www.asdreams.org (founded by Gale Delaney, psychologist)
http://www.lucidity.com (on lucid dreaming)
http://fly.to/thedreampage

On scientific research on "para-normal" abilities in the dream state, in the waking state or under hypnosis.

Dossey Larry, *Reinventing Medicine: Beyond Mind-Body To A New Era Of Healing*, New York, Haper Collins, 1999.

Woods Ralph L. and Greenhouse Herbert B., Editors, *The New World of Dreams*, New York, Macmillan Publishing Co, inc., second printing 1974, p. 273 et ss et p. 405 et ss.

NOTES

[1] On the concept of *persona* in ancient Roman law, see: *Ancient Egyptian Wisdom For The Internet,*, L'Harmattan, Paris, 2002. On the variations of the concept of person in philosophy from antiquity until today, see: Tzitzis Stamatios, *Qu'est-ce que la personne?* Paris, Armand Colin, 1999

[2] *Ever lasting Wisdom of Ancient Roman Law*, Innovative Justice, Paris, 1995, Innovjustice@aol.com

[3] Information found in Changeux Jean-Pierre, *Neuronal Man, The Biology of Mind*, New York, Oxford, Oxford University Press, 1986, Originally published in France as *L'homme Neuronal* by Fayard, Paris, 1983, p. 60. On the use of the electroencephalograph in dream laboratories, see: *The New World of Dreams*, New York, Macmillan Publishing Co, inc., second printing 1974, p. 278.

[4] According to Georges Hadjo, researches in electrography took place as early as 1900 and Semyon Kirlian was not aware of the results of his predecessors: Carsten in England and Henri BARADUC and Lodko Narkiewiez in Paris in 1896, see his

interesting article "L'effet Kirlian", in *Bio Contact*, Gaillac, France, n° 112, March 2002, biocontact@wanadoo.fr. See: Lindgren C. E. (Editor), *Capturing the Aura: Integrating Science, Technology and Metaphysics*, Blue Dolphin Pub, June 2000; Krippner Stanley and Rubin Daniel, *Kirlian Aura*, Garden City. N.Y., Doubleday & Co, 1974. *The Human Aura in Acupuncture and Kirlian Photography* (Social Change Series), By Acupuncture, and Western hemisphere Conference on Kirlian Photography, Gordon and Breach Science Pub; 1974.

[5] Some clairvoyants and healers affirm that they can see the aura, and that they can diagnose health problems through its colours. This is very interesting but unfortunately not everyone can see the aura, while dreaming is available to everyone at any time.

[6] Democritus believed that we pick up, through the skin, images emitted by objects and people. He believed that these images conveyed emotions. See: J.P. Dumont, *Les Présocratiques*, Paris, Pléïade, Folio Essai, 1988, p. 542, quoted by Jackie Pigeaud in her observations on the translation of *La Vérité des songes* by Aristotle, *op. cit.* Ancient books on dreams have not conveyed comprehensive studies about research on the connections between the tangible and

the intangible during the dreaming process. The authors of antiquity were too much focussed on dream interpretation with a practical aim and on foretelling the future. Moreover it seems that these authors, like other people, neglected their own self-observation of the dreaming process. Aristotle does not show through his writing a sound knowledge of this phenomenon. Self inner observation was not the basis of Artemidorus' works on dream interpretation. Artemidorus was very famous for his dream dictionary, (Artemidorus, *The Interpretation of Dreams: Oneirocritica*, Translated by White R. J., Park Ridge, N.J., Noyes Press, 1975). Artemidorus did not make the *third choice* which allows to consider the dreaming process in a wider life context including both the tangible and the intangible worlds. All the authors, modern or ancient, are too much focussed on the content of dreams and not enough open to the realities that would allow a better understanding of the dreaming process. In ancient Egypt, people and magicians were also interested in dreams, mainly for foretelling the future, as Wallis-Budge E. A. has stated. He also wrote that the Egyptian magicians had invented spells to get dreams on the future. He quote the Papyrus n° 122 of the British Museum, line

64 and following and line 359 and following, in his article: Wallis-Budge E. A, "Dream magic of Ancient Egypt", 129-130, *The New World of Dreams, op. cit.*

[7] In the same line, see: Dossey Larry, *Reinventing Medicine: Beyond Mind-Body To A New Era Of Healing*, New York, Harper Collins, 1999, p. 80.

[8] On the fact observed under hypnosis that the conscious mind acts as a filter, see: SNOW Chet B., Wambach Helen, Vision du futur de l'humanité, Saint Michel Editions, Saint Michel de Boulogne, France, Collection Témoignages, 1992, p. 64. Translated from the American by Christiane Joseph, original title: *Mass Dreams of the Future*, New York, Mc Graw-Hill Publishing Company,1989.

[9] Moss Robert, Dreaming True, *How to Dream Your Future and Change Your Life for the Better*, New York, Pocket Books, September 2000, p. xiii.

[10] On this topic see: Eggan Dorothy, "The Culture Shapes the Dream", p. 120-124, in *The New World of Dreams, op. cit.*

[11] For example: Chevalier Jean, Gheerbrant Alain, *Dictionnaire des Symboles*, Laffont, Jupiter, collection Bouquins, Paris, 1982. Or on the symbols of "moon" or "water" see: Eliade Mircea, *Une nouvelle philosophie de la Lune*, Paris, L'Herne, 2001.

[12] I do not advise isolation to depressed people.
[13] See question n° 1.
[14] For examples of dreams announcing death and for examples of warning dreams see: Kelsey Morton, *Dreams: A Way to Listen to God*, New York/Mahwah, Paulist Press, 1989, p. 13, p.44, p. 72, p. 74 and p.79. See also: *The New World of Dreams*, op. cit., p. 132.
[15] For a famous example that has changed the course of recent history, see: Dee Nerys, *Your Dreams and what They Mean*, London and San Francisco, Thorsons, 1984, p. 28.
[16] Galen, *On diagnosis from Dreams*, Translation by Oberhelman S. T., J. Histoire médicale 38, 1983, p. 36-47; Hippocrate, *Du Régime*, translation by Joly R., Paris, Belles Lettres, 1967.
[17] Also trains for some people.
[18] Descartes René, *Discours de la Méthode*, Paris, GF Flammarion, 1966, p 208, original text: *"Un moment après, il eut un troisième songe... il trouva un livre sur sa table, sans savoir qui l'y avait mis. Il l'ouvrit et voyant que c'était un Dictionnaire, il en fut ravi dans l'espérance qu'il pourrait lui être fort utile. Dans le même instant, il se rencontra un autre livre sous sa main, qui ne lui était pas moins nouveau, ne sachant d'où il lui était venu. Il trouva que c'était un recueil des Poésies de différents auteurs, intitulé*

Corpus Poëtarum etc. Il eut la curiosité d'y vouloir lire quelque chose: et à l'ouverture du livre, il tomba sur le vers Quod Vitae sectabor iter? (= quelle voie suivrai-je en la vie?).

[19] Moss Robert also noticed this fact, see about his dreams of visits to the gas station and its connection to money matter in reality, *Dreamgates*, op. cit., p. 303.

[20] Delaney Gale, *All About Dreams, Everything You Need to Know About Why We Have Them, What They Mean, and How To Put Them to Work for You,* New York, HarperCollins, HarperSanfrancisco, 1988, p. 104 and following.

[21] Delaney Gale, *All About Dreams, op.cit.,* p. 79.

[22] See Moss Robert's examples about psychic litter in hotels, *Dreamgates, op. cit.,* p. 216

[23] For examples quoted by a modern doctor, see: Dossey Larry, *Reinventing Medicine, op.cit.,* p. 123.

[24] Do not reject the dreams showing your defects. When you have such dreams it is because you are ready to improve yourself and the dreams encourage you to do so. Remember that we are all able of transformation.

[25] I do not advise this experiment to depressed people.

[26] Doctor Bach's floral remedies. See note n° 81.
[27] Allende Isabel, *Paula*, Paris, Fayard, 1995 French translation, original version: Paula, Barcelona, Plaza & Janès Editores, S.A., p. 153: original text in French: "Notre complicité est si totale que nos rêves se mêlent et que le lendemain nous ne savons plus qui a rêvé de quoi." See also Moss Robert, *Dreaming True*, op. cit., p. 93
[28] See Moss Robert's examples of psychic litter in hotels, *Dreamgates*, op. cit., p. 303.
[29] See for examples about Soho, and Greenwich Village: Metzger Christine, *New York*, Cologne, Könemann, 2001, p. 243.
[30] This is sometimes unpleasant when we are in touch with some people.
[31] Berberova Nina, *C'est moi qui souligne*, Translated from Russian by Anne and René MISSLIN, Paris, J'ai lu, p. 447.
[32] Some authors also noticed the same, see for example: Moss Robert, *Dreaming True, How to Dream Your Future and Change Your Life for the Better*, New York, Pocket Books, September 2000, p. 29 et p. 189; and by the same author, *Dreamgates*, p. 17-19; DEE Nerys, *Your Dreams and what They Mean*, London and San Francisco, Thorsons, 1984, p. 85.
[33] Allende Isabel, *Paula*, op.cit., p. 158. See also on dreams announcing birth:

Malinowski Bronislaw, "The dream is the Cause of the Wish", p.118-119: "Another class of typical dream is concerned with the birth of babies. In these the future mother has a sort of dream annunciation from one of her dead relatives.", in *The New World of Dreams*, *op.cit.*, p. 119.

[34] See in the Frequently asked questions, the section about psychological nightmares.

[35] Buddhist yogis have noticed that if you have a tension while in a deep sleep, this tension tends to be reproduced in the dreaming state and to induce karmic dreams. See: Norbu NamKhai, *Le Yoga du Rêve*, Paris, J.L. Accarias, 1993, collection L'originel, translation by arrangement with Snow Lion Publications, Ithaca, New York 14851.

[36] The British Doctor Edward Bach has invented remedies to help balance emotional states and heal negative emotions deemed to induce physical illnesses. His philosophy of medicine was much in advance for his time, as it took into account the role played by emotions in the formation of illness. In England one can find these remedies very easily in drugstores, pharmacies and even at the airports. In France and in America we can find them in healthy food shops. On Doctor Bach's philosophy of medicine, see: Bach Edward,

Heal Thyself, An Explanation of the Real Cause and Cure of Disease, Saffron Walden, Essex, The C.W. Daniel Company Limited, 1931. On Doctor Bach's remedies see: from the same publisher: *The Twelve Healers,* by Edward Bach. See also note n° 60. One of the most useful remedies is "rescue remedy", it helps overcome physical and psychological shocks.

[37] The enthusiasts of lucid dreaming propose to act directly in the dream state by fighting the enemies or change the course of an unpleasant dream, etc... For more information on lucid dreaming see the Frequently Asked Questions: What is a lucid dream?

[38] On this subject, see Cicero, *De divinatione*, II, LXIX, 142, Hyppocrate: Régime IV. See also about the Greek doctor Galen: Moss Robert, *Dreaming True, op. cit.*, p. 157.

[39] This may work if you believe it will.

[40] Barash Marc Ian, *Healing Dreams, Exploring The Dreams That can Transform Your Life*, New York, Riverhead Books a member of penguin Putnam Inc, 2000, this book is a testimony written by a man who began to pay attention to his dreams because he suddenly had a lot of nightmares. Thanks to his dreams he was able to help doctors in diagnosing cancer and he was saved.

[41] On drugs that suppress dreams and on the effects on dreaming of diverse drugs, alcohol, and coffee, see: *The New World of Dreams, op.cit.,* p.238 et p. 390.

[42] See for example the series of lectures on the mental process of scientific creation, Académie des Sciences Morales et Politiques en France, *Revue des Sciences Morales et Politiques*, Paris, 1987, see especially the discourses of Jean Bernard, Jean-Claude Pecker, Laurent Schwartz, François Jacob, Jean Hamburger.

[43] *Cf.* Dossey Larry, *Reinventing Medicine: Beyond Mind-Body To A New Era Of Healing*, New York, Harper Collins, 1999. This book reports all the experiences that have been made in the United States on "paranormal" phenomena, sometimes in prestigious academic institutions, such as the university of Harvard. See notably, p. 53 note 21, p. 37 and p. 47. See also on the healing effects of group prayers, p. 48. See also, quoted by the author: The Archives of Scientists' Transcendental Experiences (TASTE), http://psychology.ucdavis.edu/tart/taste ou http://www.issc-taste.org.

[44] According to Ann Kato, Vice-president of the Swiss Society for Neurosciences. See: http://www.swissup.com/art_content.cfm?u pid=FR3110

[45] *Cf* an interesting article on this subject: "Les combines de la triche high-tech", by Laurence BEAUVAIS, in *L'ordinateur Individuel*, n° 139, pp. 102-105, May 2002, www.01net.com, The author quotes the following sites: cheathouse.com and gradesaver.com and the anti-cheat site: plagiarism.com, wordcheck.com and canexus.com/eve.

[46] On this, see: Norbu NamKhai, *Le Yoga du Rêve, op.cit.*, p. 144.

[47] On telepathic abilities under hypnosis, see: Snow Chet B., Wambach Helen, *op.cit.*, p. 66 et p. 67: The researches done have proved, according to the authors that half of the people under hypnosis were able to telepathically communicate thoughts and feelings.

[48] Telepathy during the dream state has been successfully experienced in the Maimonide laboratories in New York (Division of Parapsychology and Psychophysics of Maimonides Medical Center in Brooklyn, New York). About these experiments see: *The New World of Dreams, op.cit.*, p. 273 et ss et p. 405 et ss. In the United States many other academic laboratories have effected some researches on the so-called "para-normal" abilities during the dream state and during the

waking state, see: Larry Dossey *op. cit.* passim.

[49] See the assertions of Isabel Allende regarding her grand-mother who was gifted in reading other's thoughts and "communicating with animals: Allende Isabel, *Paula*, Paris, Fayard, 1995 French translation, original version: Paula, Barcelona, Plaza & Janès Editores, S.A.,.p. 12.

[50] Greene David, *Your Incredible Cat: Understanding the Secret Powers of Your Pet*, Budget Book services, Incorporated, 1995; Steiger Brad,.*Cats incredible!: true stories of fantastic feline feats*, New York, N.Y, Plume, 1994; Steiger Brad and Steiger Sherry Hansen, *Strange Powers of Pets*, New York, DIF, Donald I. Fince, 1992. See also the bibliography of Dossey Larry, *op. cit.*, D. Badens, *Psychic Animals New York*, Barnes and Nobles, 1996; Sheldrake R. and Smart P., "Psychic Pets: A Survey in North-West England," *Society for Psychical Research 61*, 1997; Schul Bill, *The Psychic Power of Animals*, New York: FawcettA, 1977.

[51] Hiby Lydia with Weintraub S. Bonnie, *Conversations with Animals*, Troutdale, OR, NewSage Press, 1998, p.4 et p. 158.

[52] Snow Chet B., Wambach Helen, *op. cit.*, p. 66.

[53] *Ibid*, translation from the French version: "les mots sont un écran de fumée". La vraie

communication, insistait-elle, se fait télépathiquement, sous le niveau des mots."

[54] Hiby Lydia, *op.cit.*, p. 5: "The words are not my own, but rather the animal's spirit talking to my higher self" and p. 158:"But always remember that your higher self is the clearest channel for hearing an animal's voice."

[55] First, make sure you do not use medicine suppressing dreams.

[56] See: Norbu NamKhai, *Le Yoga du Rêve*, Paris, J.L. Accarias, 1993, collection L'originel, *op. cit.*, p. 75.

[57] Devereux Paul and Devereux Charla, *The Lucid Dreaming Book, How to awake within, control and use your dreams*, Boston, Tokyo, Journey Editions, 1998.

[58] SAlvatge Geneviève, *Décodez vos rêves*, Paris, Presses Pocket, 1992, p. 20-21 and 34-35.

[59] Laboratory Deva, P.P. 3, 38880 Autran, France; Dr. Edward Bach Centre Mount Vernon, Wallingford, Oxon OX10-OPZ. In the United states floral remedies can be found in healthy food shops; Dr. Bach's remedies are easy to find in the UK at chemist shops and even at airport shops. In France, they are generally sold in healthy food shops and in Paris in some specialized shops like: Anthyllide, www.anthyllide.com

[60] Garfield Patricia L., *La créativité onirique, Du rêve ordinaire au rêve lucide*, (original title *Creative Dreaming*), Paris, J'ai Lu, 1974, p. 200.
[61] Ancelin Schützenberger Anne, *Aïe mes aïeux!*, Paris, Desclée de Brouwer, 1999, p. 15, "L'hérédité archaïque de l'homme ne comporte pas que des prédispositions mais aussi des contenus idéatifs des traces mnésiques qu'ont laissées les expériences faites par les générations antérieures" (Freud Sigmund, *Moïse et le monothéisme*, 1939, Gallimard, Poche, Collection Idées, 1948, p. 134).
[62] Ancelin Schützenberger Anne, *Aïe mes aïeux!*, Paris, Desclée de Brouwer, 1999
[63] Ancelin Schützenberger Anne, *Aïe mes aïeux!*, Paris, Desclée de Brouwer, 1999, p. 64, "On constate en clinique la transmission transgénérationnelle de traumatismes graves non parlés -ou dont le deuil n'a pas été fait- comme de traumatismes de guerre (gaz, noyades ou quasi-noyades, tortures, viols - blessant un parent ou son frère ou un camarade de guerre).
Rien de ce que nous connaissons au point de vue psychologique, physiologique ou neurologique ne permet de comprendre comment quelque chose peut tracasser des générations de la même famille."

[64] In the same line, see: Moss Robert, *Dreaming True*, op. cit., p. 253.
[65] See: *The New World of Dreams*, New York, *op.cit.*, p. 154.
[66] *Ibid, The New World of Dreams*, op. cit., p.117.
[67] See p. 38.
[68] Moss Robert, *Dreamgates*, op. cit., p. 42.
[69] For example: Chevalier Jean, Gheerbrant Alain, *Dictionnaire des Symboles*, Laffont, Jupiter, collection Bouquins, Paris, 1982.
[70] On relationships between people in the dream state, see: Dossey Larry, *Reinventing Medicine: Beyond Mind-Body To A New Era Of Healing*, op. cit., p. 97.
[71] Norbu NamKhai, *Le Yoga du Rêve*, Paris, J.L. Accarias, 1993, *op.cit.*, p. 39 of the introduction and p. 70.
[72] Delaney Gale, *All About Dreams*, op. cit., p. 219.

By the same author:

How to Better Understand Ancient Civilizations
Anna Mancini, Ph. D

In all of the disciplines that regard ancient civilizations, generations of researchers have acquired treasures for which they don't have a key for understanding. Nobody will find this key through deciphering old manuscripts, digging the earth or diving deep into the ocean. This key is available to all of us, in our sub-conscience; we just need to recover it. This book explains how you can do that. Our modern mental structure bars us from the possibility of entering the logic of ancient peoples. In order to understand them, we need to get in touch with the ancient layers of our psyche within ourselves that are still alive when we dream. It is when we dream that we come closer to the mental universe of ancient peoples. This is why if you use the dream-reality technique explained in this book, you will be able to better understand the ancient civilizations you are studying. You will also easily solve many questions that are enigmas to our modern minds.

May this book help all lovers of ancient civilizations take better advantage of all of the many archaeological vestiges now available to them.

ISBN 13 : 978-1-932848-32-8 Ancient Civilization ppbk/ 19 USD
ISBN 13 : 978-1-932848-33-5 Ancient civilization Hard/50 USD
ISBN 13 : 978-1-932848-34-2 Ancient civilization dustjacket blue/55 USD
ISBN 13 : 978-1-932848-38-0 Ancient Civilizaiton E-book/ 7 USD

Maat Revealed,
Philosophy of Justice in Ancient Egypt
Anna Mancini Ph. D

Unlike ancient Rome, Egypt did not transmit any legal system to us, but rather an idea of justice our modern minds can hardly understand. In the ancient Egyptian world, almost all the texts and inscriptions speak of justice. All the texts of wisdom teach that one has to conform to Maat, an obscure and omnipresent concept that Egyptologists have translated into the expression "Goddess of Truth and Justice".

Egyptian justice is so different from ours that Egyptologists and historians of religions believe they have not yet fully understood its meaning. They regret this fact because understanding Maat would be a gateway to a deeper understanding of the ancient Egyptian world. As for lawyers, they have limited themselves to the Greco-Roman sources on the philosophy of Justice and the discoveries of Egyptologists in this philosophical field remain thoroughly ignored. Thanks to her experience in ancient history of law and her ability to understand ancient symbols, the author provides Egyptology with the missing pieces that were needed to form a coherent image of Maat. Once revealed, Maat sheds a new and unexpected light on the whole of Egyptian civilization. As a bridge between traditionally separate fields of academic research, this book is a useful and groundbreaking contribution to Egyptology, the history of religions and the modern philosophy of law.

ISBN : 978-1-932848-29-8 (Hardcover)
ISBN: 978-1-932848-31-1 (dusjacket)
ISBN : 978-1-932848-30-4 (Paperback)

www.ingramcontent.com/pod-product-compliance
Lightning Source LLC
Chambersburg PA
CBHW032007080426
42735CB00007B/532